A WORLD OF
PRAYER

A WORLD OF
PRAYER

EDITED BY NAOMI STARKEY

PRAYING WITH
WOMEN'S WORLD DAY OF PRAYER

Text copyright © Women's World Day of Prayer 2005
Musical notation copyright © David Wilkinson 2005
The author asserts the moral right
to be identified as the author of this work

Published by
The Bible Reading Fellowship
First Floor, Elsfield Hall
15–17 Elsfield Way, Oxford OX2 8FG

ISBN 1 84101 369 2
First published 2005
10 9 8 7 6 5 4 3 2 1 0
All rights reserved

A catalogue record for this book is available from the British Library

Printed and bound in Great Britain by
Bookmarque, Croydon

CONTENTS

WOMEN'S WORLD DAY OF PRAYER

With the motto 'Informed prayer and prayerful action', Women's World Day of Prayer is a worldwide movement of Christian women, from many church traditions, who come together to observe a common day of prayer on the first Friday in March each year.

The Day of Prayer begins as dawn breaks over the islands of Tonga in the Pacific and continues in a great 'Mexican wave' of prayer reaching countries like Fiji and New Zealand. It continues through Asia in countries such as Japan, the Philippines, Korea and Bangladesh. It rolls on to the countries of Africa, including Egypt, and then to the Middle East. It continues on to Europe, east and west. Crossing the Atlantic, it goes to the Caribbean, South, Central, and North America and on to the Pacific again, until the last services of the day are held on the island of Samoa.

The roots of the Day of Prayer are back in 1887 when the wife of a Presbyterian minister in New York, and mother of seven, Mary Ellen James, was moved by the problems faced by many women around her, particularly new immigrants to America—poverty, unemployment, poor housing, and lack of health and educational facilities. She decided to call together the women of her church for a day of prayer, 'where there shall be confession of individual and national sins with offerings that fitly express the contrition'.

Mary Ellen James did not intend to start a worldwide movement, but by 1919 Women's World Day of Prayer had come into being, uniting her initiative with a day of prayer for overseas missions begun by two Baptist missionaries appalled by the deprivation of women in many other parts of the world.

News of this special day began to spread, and the first service was held in Scotland in 1930, in England in 1932, in Wales in 1933 and in Ireland two years later. The movement grew dramatically after World War II and by 1968 no fewer than 127 countries were taking part. The work is now overseen by an international committee, comprising representatives of all national committees and meeting approximately every four years to choose themes and writers for future services.

Themes are allocated to countries that have expressed a desire to prepare an order of service. When the draft service order is sent out worldwide, each national committee can, if necessary, amend it slightly to ensure its suitability for their particular country. It is translated into more than 60 languages and 1000 dialects.

An international executive committee takes care of more detailed planning for the day, made up of representatives of the eight regions of the world—Africa, Asia, Caribbean, Europe, Latin America, Middle East, North America and Pacific. All money received in the offerings, which form part of the service, is used to support the prayer movement and for Christian literature and educational projects.

In England, Wales and Northern Ireland, there are over 3000 Women's World Day of Prayer branches, holding around 5000 services involving thousands of people—not only women, but men and children as well.

For further information contact:
Women's World Day of Prayer
Commercial Road
Tunbridge Wells
Kent TN1 2RR

Tel: 01892 541411
E-mail: office@wwdp-natcom.org
Websites: www.wwdp-natcomm.org *and* www.worlddayofprayer.net

HOW TO USE
A WORLD OF PRAYER

This book is compiled from some of the orders of service prepared for Women's World Day of Prayer over recent years, with each chapter featuring a different theme and country. The same basic structure is followed each time, with some slight variations—introductory background material, followed by a welcome, a call to worship, prayers of confession, intercession, thanksgiving and dedication (some using a dramatized format, some using simple music), Bible readings, imaginative exercises for personal or communal response, and a final blessing.

If you are looking for material for a small group, you could use either all or part of a chapter to enrich a time of prayer and worship, adapting it as necessary to fit your group size and requirements. The liturgies could also work well as part of a group quiet day or retreat programme, or you could simply read through the services on your own, blending your personal prayers with those of women around the world.

For use in a whole-church context, you could add your own choice of worship songs and also a talk based around the theme to make a full-length service. Alternatively, as with smaller groups, you could select and adapt parts of the liturgies to use for times of intercession, for a drama presentation, for focusing on a theme such as justice, healing or caring for creation, or even for an internationally themed service celebrating a particular country.

Note: Every reasonable effort has been made to check that the introductory background material is up to date, but it may be subject to change, especially in countries with volatile political situations. We suggest you check the internet to make sure of the latest information, where necessary.

GOD'S PEOPLE: INSTRUMENTS OF HEALING

Guatemala

BACKGROUND

The women of Guatemala have a strong sense of community. They share with us their recognition that the church is a living organism, concerned with human conditions and able to initiate the process of change and healing.

Guatemala is a mountainous country where the northern plains and Pacific seaboard enjoy a tropical climate, moderated by temperate seas. In the western mountains it is cold, with warmer, fertile river valleys. Among its mountains are 33 volcanic peaks and innumerable beautiful lakes. With this wide variety of climate and habitat, it is not surprising that the country is rich in flora and fauna, particularly orchids, the national flower. The national symbol is the brightly coloured Quetzal bird with its unique characteristic of being unable to live in captivity.

Guatemala is the cradle of the Maya civilization, which excelled in science and mathematics, particularly as applied to architecture, engineering and astronomy. It was the Maya who first developed a system of hieroglyphics and manufactured paper and books. They also had great artistic qualities, shown in their music, paintings, ceramics and pottery. The national book of the Quiché people, which embodies their great mythological legacy, is one of the rarest relics of aboriginal thought.

The Maya were unknown to most of the rest of the world until 500 years ago, yet now archaeologists and scholars are discovering the richness of their culture. After Columbus opened up the Americas to exploration, these lands were ruled by the Spanish until the independence of Central America in 1821. Later, Guatemala became an independent nation.

Guatemala is a multi-cultural country but is unique in Central America because of the high percentage of indigenous people, who still preserve their own language, customs, traditions and original dress. These people live mainly in the west, and the women weave fabrics for their beautiful and distinctive costumes.

The native culture is rich in artistic expression of all kinds but there are also contemporary artists, musicians and writers who have achieved worldwide acclaim. The official language is Spanish but the indigenous peoples also have their own languages and dialects.

Although Guatemala is a secular state, its constitution protects freedom of religion. The majority of the population is considered Catholic but traditional beliefs and practices also persist and there are considerable numbers of sects and faiths.

In spite of the natural beauties of Guatemala and the richness of its heritage, there have been many obstacles to overcome. The high level of illiteracy and infant mortality, the rapidly expanding population, urbanization and crime have all led to deterioration in the quality of life. These problems must be solved before the children can be offered a better tomorrow.

WELCOME

Leader: Dear sisters and brothers, members of the whole of God's family, the Christian women of Guatemala invite you to unite with them in prayer, praying that we will all be used by God as instruments of healing.

Guatemala is the cradle of a great civilization, the Mayan civilization. The Maya excelled in the fields of mathematics, architecture, engineering, astronomy and the fine arts. The Maya were experts in agriculture and they discovered and perfected their own means of subsistence. They had great knowledge of plants, especially medicinal ones, which they used effectively for healing the sick. These plants are still used in medicine today. The Maya were also known for a profound sense of family unity, which they continue to cherish. A strong sense of solidarity is very much part of Mayan culture; it allowed them to develop a communal life and greatly aided in the evolution of their traditions. The Maya say, 'Let all get up, let all be called; let there not be one or two groups among us that lag behind.'

Please turn to your neighbour with words of welcome and friendship.

CALL TO WORSHIP

Leader: Come, let us praise the Lord.

All: O come, let us sing to the Lord;
Let us make a joyful noise to the rock of our salvation!
Let us come into his presence with thanksgiving;
Let us make a joyful noise to him with songs of praise.
For the Lord is a great God,
and a great King above all gods.
(PSALM 95:1–3, NRSV)

Leader: God, our heavenly Father, we draw near to you with thankful hearts because of your great love for us. We thank you most of all for the gift of your dear Son, in whom alone we may be one. We are different from one another in race and language, in material things, in gifts, in opportunities, but each of us has a human heart, knowing joy and sorrow, pleasure and pain. We are one in our need of your forgiveness, your strength, your love; make us one in our response to you, that bound by common love, and freed from selfish aims, we may work for the good of all and the advancement of your kingdom.

The women of Guatemala speak:

Reader: Guatemala is a small, beautiful country of only eight million inhabitants. It is considered a paradise in the heart of the Americas but it is physically and spiritually sick. It is a country exhausted by immense social problems and by sin. Our country is very rich in natural resources but suffers from immense misery and poverty. There is a high rate of infant mortality. There is a shortage of housing and basic goods. There is a poor education system with a high rate of illiteracy, disorientated young people, delinquency, violence of all kinds, drugs, alcoholism and abandoned children. There is hardly any assistance for those who are elderly or handicapped.

It would not be just or honest if we only enumerated the social problems that overwhelm us. The church is alive and concerned about these problems and is making efforts in the urban and rural areas to find possible solutions. Our world is in ruins and it is an arduous task to know where to begin. If we do not bring about changes in all social areas, the little we can do will simply ease the situation, not cure it. We believe that some things are being accomplished but we need to co-ordinate our efforts to make a greater impact.

Faced with the situation we have tried to describe,

for us, the women of Guatemala, the crucial question is, 'How can we proclaim ourselves to be the people of God, to be used as instruments of healing?'

May God grant us the illumination of the Holy Spirit as we pray together. May God help us find solutions for our problems.

Leader: It is from this situation that the women of Guatemala invite us to join them in asking God to make us all become 'The People of God: Instruments of Healing'.

We come before you, Lord, asking that you will bind us together in love with our sisters and brothers throughout the world. Through Jesus your Son we experience healing of our souls by his suffering on the cross. Grant us the grace to see the needs of others and the courage to act accordingly, that others may see in us the love and compassion that Jesus showed in his ministry. May Christ's touch be upon us, that we may truly be 'The People of God: Instruments of Healing'.

Silence.

Leader: The apostle Peter wrote: 'Like good stewards of the manifold grace of God, serve one another with whatever gift each of you has received. Whoever speaks must do so as one speaking the very words of God; whoever serves must do so with the strength that God supplies.' *(1 Peter 4:11, NRSV)*

All: In everything may God receive the glory, through Jesus Christ, since to God alone belongs all glory and power for ever and ever. Amen.

PRAYERS OF CONFESSION

Leader: O God, we confess to you that we have lost the vision of the first Christians. We have been selfishly accepting all the benefits that come from you, forgetting those by our side who are in greater need.

All: Forgive us, O God.

Leader: We have not been a community-minded church: we have lacked the kind of solidarity in which the early church excelled. We confess we are not yet of one accord.

All: Forgive us, O God.

Leader: O God, we confess that we have sinned against you in thought, word and deed. We have not sought your face in the face of our neighbour. We confess with our Guatemalan sisters that we have been insensitive to the pain of others; to the plight of orphans, the poverty of widows, the suffering of abandoned children, the despair of refugees and homeless people, the anguish of drug abusers and AIDS sufferers. We have remained blind and deaf to the cries of those who beg for our help.

All: Forgive us, O God.

Leader: O God, we pray we may be awakened from our indifference and apathy and become caring and compassionate.

All: Create in me a clean heart, O God; and renew a right spirit within me.

14

BIBLE READING
Acts 3:1–13a, 15b–16

PRAYING VOICES FROM GUATEMALA

Reader: Juana speaks: Jesus always showed interest in individuals: he gave sight to the blind, made the paralysed walk, freed the captives, healed all kinds of sickness, liberated those possessed by the devil, gave food to the hungry, and comforted the afflicted and broken-hearted.

All: Lord, heal us all.

Reader: Maria speaks: There are so many sick people without money to buy medicine, and every day it becomes more expensive. Many children are malnourished because the money their parents earn is not enough for the bare necessities of life.

In Guatemala, it is frightening to see the number of abandoned children who walk the streets, without food or clothing, without a home, education, or family care. At present we call them 'street children'. We do not care enough for widows and orphans, or for those who are handicapped or elderly. In the name of Jesus, help us all to become a Christian community showing love and compassion to those around us.

All: Lord, heal us all.

Reader: Rosa speaks: We recognize that young people every-where have enormous potential. Yet we see with immense sadness that without guidance and knowledge

of Jesus they often seek satisfaction in alcohol and
drugs. Lead us, Lord, so that we are able to offer our
young people a way of life that fulfils their needs and
helps them to follow in your way.

All: Lord, heal us all.

Reader: Clara speaks: We pray that the leaders of all nations
will serve the people they represent with responsibility
and understanding. Give them wisdom to govern with
justice and to work for the good of their people, so that
hunger and misery, destruction and desolation may be
eliminated, and peace become a reality.

All: Lord, heal us all.

Reader: Josefina speaks: Jesus, thank you for the gift of faith,
and your gracious love in our own lives. Help us to see
people in need with the eyes of compassion, identifying
problems, reaching over barriers and showing our love
and concern. May your love flow through us, touching
those around us. Help us to be your people—
instruments for healing.

All: Lord, heal us all.

Reader: Carmen speaks: O God, we rely on your mercy which
never fails. Give us confidence in your power to heal
and save, and to satisfy the needs of all your people. 'In
you we live and move and have our being', and so,
wherever your people are to be found, there you are...
    in the far corners of the world,
    in every continent and island,
    bringing relief to human misery and pain.
Every day, help us to become instruments of love and

healing, through word and deed. We offer our prayer in Jesus' name.

All: Amen.

GREETING OF PEACE

Leader: When we read in the Gospels of the many miracles performed by Jesus, we notice how often Jesus touched a sick person. When we look back at the recorded history of the early Christian community, we can see their struggle to understand how they were to carry on the message and ministry of Jesus. We read in a letter of John that 'love is not to be just words or mere talk, but something real and active'. *(1 John 3:18, JB)*

In fact, they were recognized as followers of Jesus because of their love for one another. Before we extend the greeting of peace, we ask you to use this moment of silence to think about what part of yourself you would like to be healed… *[pause]*

Please think about your community… *[pause]* your town or city… *[pause]* your family… *[pause]*. Where can you be an instrument of healing? *[pause]*

Please stand. Now turn and hold your neighbour's hand and say to each other, 'In the name of Jesus, be healed and become an instrument of healing.'

PRAYER OF THANKSGIVING AND DEDICATION

A large globe is carried forward (or a map of the world can be substituted) by a group of people, in such a way that the congregation sees the world being held tenderly by the people of God. The map or globe does not need to be lifted high. It is more important that everyone sees in this gesture that the world is being entrusted to the people of God.

All: Lord, we thank you for our world—for its infinite varieties of people, colours, races and cultures, for the endless opportunities of making new relationships, venturing across new frontiers, creating new things, discovering new truths, healing the hurt and the broken.

Forgive us for our narrowness of vision which sees only the clouds and misses the rainbow. Amen.

Leader: Now we invite you to think about a place in the world that you know needs God's healing. Recall what you know about this place, its problems, its pains, its difficulties. Think about the people there who are suffering and those who are trying to help them. As you think about the world, open your hands in front of you with your palms facing upward, as if you were holding it in your hands.

Silence.

Leader: Let us pray.

Jesus, you have listened to our petitions in which we have expressed our concerns and worries about the evil that reigns in the world. We thank you that you grant us the privilege of being used as instruments, as your hands, so as to be able to make your promises a beautiful reality. It is our deepest prayer that we shall grow nearer to the happy day in which we will be able to say in unison, 'The Lord is my shepherd, nothing shall I want.'

Give us, Father, a vision of your world as love would make it: a world where the weak are protected and none go hungry; a world whose benefits are shared, so that everyone can enjoy them; a world whose different people and cultures live with tolerance and mutual respect; a world where peace is built with justice and justice is fired with love; and give us the courage to build it. Through Jesus Christ our Lord.

All: Amen.

BLESSING

All: The Lord bless us and keep us, the Lord make his face to shine upon us and be gracious unto us, the Lord lift up the light of his countenance upon us and give us his peace, now and for ever. Amen.

2

THE EARTH IS A HOUSE
FOR ALL PEOPLE

Ghana

BACKGROUND

Ghana, in West Africa, is a beautiful country with many attractive natural features. The climate ranges from hot and humid in the south-west to warm and less humid in the north. After British colonization in 1821, the country became known as Gold Coast. On Independence, the country was named Ghana, taking the name of one of the old kingdoms of the ancient empire.

Contact with Europe began in the 15th century, firstly with the Portuguese, then the Dutch, British and Danish. The British took control from their fellow Europeans in the mid-1870s, and established political rule until Independence in 1957. After a series of coups, the constitution was suspended in 1981, but in 1992 a new constitution was approved, restoring multi-party politics.

There are many ethnic groups in Ghana, with their own indigenous languages, although the official language is English. Women have equal rights with men, although illiteracy among women means that they are not always aware of their rights. The extended family system means that individuals are cared for within their own family and that returning 'exiles' are not a burden on society.

There are three main religious groups. Sixty per cent are Christian of various denominations and churches. Thirteen per cent are Muslims and 23 per cent are members of the Traditional Religions. The Church has pioneered in many fields, educational, social, economic and medical, and is still committed to many of these areas. It is constantly concerned with the problem of refugees, as people have fled conflict situations in other West African countries.

The main economic activities in Ghana are farming, small-scale cottage industry and mining. The chief commercial products are cocoa, timber, gold, diamonds, bauxite, manganese and aluminium. In spite of a large reservoir of both human and mineral resources forming the basis of its former economic prosperity, since 1966 there has been a deterioration in the situation, bringing hardship to vulnerable groups in society.

WELCOME

Leader: In Ghana, a greeting means more than just 'Hello'. To greet someone is a way of affirming or acknowledging that you have met a fellow human being. The meaning that is conveyed in this simple exchange is tremendous: you and I belong to one human family. The women in Ghana greet us using three of their languages and so we greet each other in this way.

For each greeting their response is 'Yoo' *[pronounced as written]*, meaning 'Yes, I accept your warm greetings.'

And so I greet you in the Akan language: 'Akwaaba' *[pronounced A QuaBa]*.

All: 'Yoo.'

Leader: In the Ewe language: 'Mia—woezo' *[pronounced Mia Wozoo]*.

21

All: 'Yoo.'

Leader: In the Dangme language: 'Moyee' *[pronounced Maw ye]*.

All: 'Yoo.'

Leader: The people of Ghana invite you, the people of all nations and languages, to join in worship for the whole world.

    We come together in the presence of God, Creator and Sustainer of the whole universe, to reflect on the fact that the earth is a house given by God to all people as their home. We are here to praise him and thank him for his love and care, to confess our sins for the way we have selfishly misused the earth so graciously given to us, and to resolve, through the power of the Holy Spirit, to do better, to renew the earth and to bring peace in our generation and in generations to come.

CALL TO WORSHIP

Leader: When I look at your heavens, the work of your fingers, the moon and the stars that you have established, what are human beings that you are mindful of them, mortals that you care for them? Yet you have made them a little lower than God and crowned them with glory and honour. *(Psalm 8:3–6, NRSV)*

OPENING PRAYER AND PRAISE

Leader: Let us praise God for his greatness and majesty, for his love and wisdom in creating us in his image and giving us the whole world as a house to live in. O Lord, our God, your greatness is seen in all the world! Your praise reaches up to the heavens.

We praise and thank you, God, for making this earth a dwelling place for us. You give us all that can make life enjoyable, birds of the air, the beasts of the field, the fish in the sea, plants and flowers which provide us with food, medicine and shelter. You ask us to take good care of them and to be each other's keeper.

All: We praise you, O God, and we acknowledge you to be the loving creator of the whole universe.

Leader: Let us praise and thank God for the ability to be wise, knowledgeable, skilful and creative. If we use these gifts wisely, then technology and science can make life on earth easier in many ways. Through better communications, we bring distant lands and their people into our homes. We can recognize ourselves as one human family and respond by sharing our lives together as God's family on this earth.

All: We praise you, O God, and we acknowledge you to be the loving creator of the whole universe.

Leader: Through the knowledge that has come to us from medical research, we have hope for preserving good drinking water and for curing and eradicating diseases such as malaria. We thank you, O God, for the wisdom you have given us in the use of herbs for food and medicine. Give us courage and wisdom to explore your creation in a responsible way so that our skills and knowledge will be used for your glory.

All: We praise you, O God, and we acknowledge you to be the loving creator of the whole universe.

DRAMA

The Prodigal Son (Luke 15:11–32)

Narrator: This story, recorded in St Luke's Gospel chapter 15, was told by Jesus and is loved by many people all over the world. It tells of a child demanding independence, a parent resisting but relenting, and an elder brother jealous and resenting the loving forgiveness of his father.

In Ghana it would be rude for a son to ask a father to give him his inheritance while the father is still alive. It would even be interpreted that the son wants his father to die early so that he can inherit his property. Anyone who inherits property in a traditional Ghanaian family is only a custodian of that property. He is supposed to share with the rest of the family. It means that the family should stick together and help each other. In this story, the son breaks the family tie, leaving them unhappy. He squanders his money and returns with nothing. Even though he had offended the tradition of community and family, and had disgraced his family's good name by his bad behaviour before the world, he still remains a member of the family.

Father: My beloved Kofi, where is your elder brother, Kojo?

Kofi: Kojo has been gone a long time to the farm with the labourers.

Father: Why didn't you go to the other cocoa farm with the farm workers? You know that your brother supervises one farm and you the other.

Kofi: Father, I am just fed up with this village life. Going to the farm, coming back in the evening to sleep, without any entertainment, makes life boring. I want to go to the city.

Father: *(To himself)* What is this that Kofi, my son whom I have loved and cherished so much, wants to do?
(Turning back to his son) Kofi, what has come over you? Are you not happy with us any more? What do you want me to do for you? I want you to be happy.

Kofi: Just give me my share of the inheritance and I shall be happy. I want to live in the city and live my life the way I want to!

Father: Kofi, did I hear you correctly? What did you say?

Kofi: I said, give me my share of the inheritance.

Father: What a request! Why are you making this demand? Are you all right? Speak up!

Kofi: I am serious, Father. There is nothing wrong with me. Just give me my share and let me go. I am bored with the village life, that's all.

Father: You know I have to consult the elders. Come back tomorrow.

Narrator: The following day Kofi returns for an answer.

Kofi: Well, Father, what have the elders said?

Father: In our culture, you can only inherit my property when I am no more. The elders met and do not approve your request. If you force me to give you your share of the property, you shall have it, but remember that you will have broken the family tie and will have to bear the consequences later.

Kofi: I am bored with all this talk of family ties and waiting.

Narrator: Sadly the father gave Kofi the property and he went off to the city. He was very popular and made many friends quickly because he was free with his money. He bought expensive clothes and gifts for his many friends. After a while, he realized that his money was all gone, and he tried to borrow from them, but when they found he was penniless, they quickly dropped him.

Now Kofi was forced to sell his clothes and other property to buy food and pay his rent. Soon he had nothing but the clothes he wore, and had to vacate his room. He managed to find badly-paying jobs, but his employers often treated him roughly. One day he realized that even the servants in his father's house were living much better than he was. He knew that he had offended his father and he could no longer claim to be his father's child. But it struck him that he might get a job as a servant.

In the meantime, his father still hoped and prayed that Kofi would return. One morning he spotted a bedraggled man coming towards the house. On a closer look, he found it was Kofi. He ran all the way to meet him and hugged him. His father, by forgiving the child who had wished him to die, gives us a very powerful example of wholeness, the right relationship between father and child.

Kofi: Father, I have sinned against heaven and against you. I am no longer worthy to be called your child.

Father: Ama, my daughter, come quickly. Kofi is home. Go and prepare water for his bath. Bring out my best kente cloth and my sandals and put them on him.

Take this ring for his finger, Kwame, go and get the fattest calf and kill it so that we may have a feast, for Kofi was dead but is now alive. He was lost but has been found.

A table could be set up with all the things ready for the congregation during the Love Feast. See pages 33–34 for more details.

Narrator: While the feast is going on, Kojo, the elder brother comes back from the farm.

Kojo: What is going on in the house? Have we got visitors?

Servant: Visitors indeed! It is your brother, Kofi, who has come back, and your father has ordered a banquet for him.

Kojo: Indeed! I must be imagining things. Didn't he take all his share of the inheritance with him? Nothing belongs to him in this house any more. Anyway, they can go on with their party, I'm not going to be part of it.

Narrator: The father, on hearing about the attitude of his elder son, comes out to plead with him.

Father: Kojo, please come in and join us. Your brother, Kofi, is back. He is changed and humble.

Kojo: Father, what are you saying? You don't mean I should come out and rejoice with Kofi, when he has squandered all his inheritance while I have been slaving for you all these years? Father, you have never given me a young goat to slaughter and enjoy with my friends. Why should you kill the fattest calf for that rascal who wasted all your wealth?

Father: Listen, my child, you are always with me and all I have is yours. But we have to celebrate and be glad because Kofi, my child and your brother, was dead and is alive again. He was lost and now he is found. Oh Kojo, we are a family again. Let us be happy together.

PRAYING VOICES FROM THE DRAMA

Kofi: I thank you, God, that my father never forgot me but was always yearning for me to return home where I truly belong. As a prodigal child, I did things that disrupted the peace in my family and community. I know now that you created this lovely world for us to enjoy. You want us to live together in it as one family. Yet, some of us are greedy and selfish and want more than our fair share of what you have provided, while others have less or nothing. We pray that, at such times, you will let your Holy Spirit convince us of our sins and that we will seek forgiveness from you.

Kojo: Lord God, I confess that I have not sought to live in close relationship with you and my fellow human beings. When I look at the world, I see that there are wars because of our thirst for power and our irresponsible use of it. Many people have become refugees, deprived of a portion of the earth they can call a home. Because of greed, we are unable to share the resources that you have abundantly provided for all of us on this earth. Because of lack of sensitivity, we are unable to understand the hurts and the pains we inflict on one another. Grant us, O Lord, hearts that are daily repentant and sensitive to the needs of others.

Father: I thank you, God, for answering my prayer. My child who was lost is returned to me. I thank you for the power to forgive. Lord, you are loving and ever ready to forgive the sinner who repents. Give us the grace that will always enable us to forgive those who wrong us and grieve us, for it is in pardoning that we are pardoned.

Narrator: Now, my brothers and sisters, join me to thank and praise God.

All: Make us your instruments of peace. Where there is strife or division, enable us, by your Holy Spirit, to bring about love, reconciliation, unity and peace. You are a God of peace. Help us to make this earth a house for all people. We ask this in the name of Jesus Christ, our Lord. Amen.

PRAYING WITH THE PEOPLE OF GHANA

Leader: In Ghana, the traditional family is the large extended family, made up of several nuclear families who trace their descent from a common ancestor. Its strength lies in its caring role, ensuring that all members play their part to make the family strong and united. This inherent concern for the welfare and dignity of each member helped to avert a national catastrophe when more than a million Ghanaians were absorbed back into the community after being expelled from Nigeria.

Voice 1: When famine came to Ghana, many people went to nearby countries. I had to leave my wife and family in our native village and make the tough journey to Nigeria but, because of the language barrier and the lack of proper arrangements, our reception was poor. I was lucky to get a job but, as more and more Ghanaians arrived, Nigeria's economy was under strain and many were unemployed. There was talk of repatriation, and fear grew. The return journey was even more traumatic and we arrived back weary and destitute, but the country welcomed us warmly and provided us with everything we needed. When I arrived in my home village, there was a great feast of thankfulness as we talked about our experiences. We were together now and able to share what we had.

Leader: O Father, we remember all those who are suffering from want and famine. Help us to give generously to those in need.

All: Hear us, O Lord.

Voice 2: I am a Liberian from Monrovia. In 1990, civil war broke out in my country. Bombed out of my home and wounded, I escaped to Ghana. Starving and suffering from my wounds, I was received into a Ghanaian family. Understanding my plight, they nursed me back to health. As the number of refugees increased, the government, together with the United Nations High Commission for Refugees, set up a camp. Food, health care and education were provided. Thanks to a scholarship, I am now educated and hope to get a job. Please pray that I do.

Leader: O Father, we remember all who suffer or are dispossessed through civil war. Help us to see all men and women as our brothers and sisters.

All: Hear us, O Lord.

Voice 3: I am a girl from Togo—a country in political turmoil. One night, my mother decided to send my sister and me away to Accra, where our concerned relatives received us with open arms and gave us food and clothing. Many others came to Accra and our family extended to 20 people. The churches helped all the exiles register as refugees.

One of my aunts gave me a sewing machine and I found work as a seamstress and so earned money for that family. I pray that one day we may all go back to Togo.

Leader: O Lord, we pray for all refugees, that they may find a welcoming community in their country of exile; and that governments may have the will to create the conditions for their return to their own lands.

All: Hear us, O Lord.

PRAYERS OF CONFESSION

Leader: Let us reflect in silence on our own community—our strengths and our failings...

O Lord our God, we often fail to see each other's needs.

All: In love and mercy, forgive us.

Leader: O Lord our God, we have used differences in race, culture, social status and religion to create walls that separate us from others, causing them hurt.

All: In love and mercy, forgive us.

Leader: O Lord our God, we acknowledge that although we profess to follow Jesus Christ, who by his death broke through barriers of hostility and enmity, we continue to be divided. Through our divisions we have weakened our witness to your love in the world.

All: In love and mercy, forgive us.

Leader: O Lord our God, we thank you that in Jesus Christ and through the power of your Holy Spirit, you are ready to forgive us our sins and draw us to yourself and to others in fellowship. Grant us, we pray, the sensitivity of your Spirit, and strengthen us so that we may live in peace and harmony as your people on this earth.

PRAYERS OF COMMITMENT

Leader: Let us each make our personal commitment to God.

All: Father, I have heard the story of the prodigal son and I have found myself to be like him in many ways. I have broken your heart by running away from you and my neighbours in the community. I rededicate myself to you. Help me to be at peace with you and my neighbours.

Leader: And now we make a united commitment to our neighbours.

All: As a community, we should 'finish with lying and tell our neighbour the truth, for we are not separate units but intimately related to each other in Christ... Let there be no more resentment, no more anger or temper, no more violence or self-assertiveness, no more slander and no more malicious remarks. Be kind to each other; be understanding. Be as ready to forgive others as God, for Christ's sake, has forgiven us' (*Ephesians 4:25, 31–32*).

LOVE FEAST (SEE NOTE ON PAGE 34)

Leader: The father gave a feast to welcome his son back into the family. A love feast is a celebration of unity with one another. Sometimes a love feast is used as an act of reconciliation. Let us, in silence, bring to God anything that separates us from our family, our church or our community.

Silent prayer.

Leader: Lord, hear our prayers.

All: In love and mercy, forgive us.

Leader: We are followers of the Lord Jesus Christ. In him we are brothers and sisters. As a sign of unity, we will shake hands with our neighbours.

As the father celebrated the return and reconciliation of his prodigal son, so we celebrate together our recognition that the earth is a house for all people and that through Christ we are reconciled to one another—whatever our many differences—and to God. So let us share this food together.

BLESSING

All: May the peace and joy of the Holy Spirit fill our hearts
and minds, and may the same Spirit grant us courage to
live a life that promotes love and well-being on the earth
now and always. Amen.

NOTE: THE LOVE FEAST

The Love Feast or *Agape* originated in the early Church and is
mentioned in the New Testament (Acts 2:6). It soon fell out of
regular use but, over the centuries, has been revived from time to
time. In the Moravian Church, it has been an accepted form of
service since the mid-18th century. It was used in the early
Methodist Church as a special private occasion where members
could give their testimonies. The central part of the service is a very
simple meal (whatever is suitable for the gathering and the place),
served and eaten in the church with quiet reverence. The person
presiding sits, as it were, at the head of the family gathered together
to discuss and think about family matters—in other words, the
things of God.

The Love Feast can be used for different purposes. Churches use
it for celebrations, thanksgivings and anniversaries, but also for
penitence and reconciliation. Sometimes it is used as a service of
fellowship and meditation, preceding a Communion service.

3

GOD CALLS US TO RESPOND

Haiti

BACKGROUND

The Republic of Haiti and the Dominican Republic make up the island of Hispaniola—the second largest island in the Caribbean. Mountains, valleys and rivers are all part of the rich and varied nature of this earthly tropical paradise, which Christopher Columbus named 'The Garden of Eden' when he discovered it in 1492. Haiti was ruled by Spain, England and then France from 1697. In 1804 it became the first black-led republic in the New World, after nearly half a million slaves joined in a revolt under the leadership of Toussaint L'Ouverture. The official langages are French and Creole.

Many presidents have been in office throughout the turbulent history of Haiti. In 1994 American troops were sent in to help restore President Aristide to his elected office. Acts of brutal violence were perpetuated right in front of the peace-keeping forces, who were helpless to intervene. In early 2004, President Aristide was ousted in an uprising, and an interim government was established.

Women play a very important part in Haitian society. They are the mainstay of both domestic and economic life. Because of this, in recent years, physical and sexual violence have been used against them as a form of political repression.

Eighty per cent of the population live in poverty. Unemployment is very high, illiteracy is high, and life expectancy is low. Haiti is one of the poorest countries in the Western hemisphere

Deforestation and bad management of natural resources have caused erosion of good farming land, and many people have had to move from the rural communities to the large cities and even abroad to find a living.

Christianity is the main religion—about 80 per cent are Roman Catholic, and 10 per cent Protestant—but many people are involved in voodoo.

INTRODUCTION

Leader: In developing the theme of this service, 'God calls us to respond', the Haitian women focus attention on how God has called people in the Bible, particularly Jeremiah and Mary. It is interesting to note that both of them were young and their respective inner struggles were played out in times of political upheaval. Their responses to God's call were the key to God's action on behalf of people who were suffering and in need. In listening to the call of God and responding to it, we must remember other countries which have similar problems to those of Haiti.

CALL TO WORSHIP

Leader: Lord our God, Father of our Lord Jesus Christ and Father of us all, we bow down before your holy presence to adore you and to offer you the praises of our hearts.

We recognize your grandeur, O God! It is you who have created the heavens, the earth, the world and those who dwell in it.

With one heart, we thank you for all your goodness, for the gift of life, for your mercy, and for the gift of your Son, Jesus Christ, who came to save us.

To you be the glory, to you be the praise, to you be thanksgiving, merciful God, for all eternity. Amen.

PRAYERS OF CONFESSION

Leader: Let us pray.

All: Lord, our God, help us to approach you with respect. You are a holy God, an all-powerful God; your majesty rises above the heavens. You have created us in your image; you have made us a little lower than the angels; you have given us rule over the works of your hands. But what have we done with the trust you have placed in us?

Leader: By our rebellion we have tarnished your image in us and have broken our communion with you and with our brothers and sisters.

All: Pardon us, Lord.

Leader: We have abused your creation; we have been stewards who deserve to be driven from your vineyard. In your mercy, you invite us continually to respond but alas, we are blinded by our selfishness, our indifference, our hypocrisy, our lack of love.

All: Pardon us, Lord.

Leader: For our indifference and carelessness toward those who are hungry and thirsty, those in despair and destitution, those who have been persecuted because of their political or religious convictions...

All: Pardon us, Lord.

Leader: For all the superstitious, evil and immoral practices by which we have made ourselves guilty before you and our neighbour; for the violence and hatred in our hearts...

All: Pardon us, Lord.

Leader: Lord, our God, we are overcome by the suffering of your children. We pray for the conversion of oppressors.

All: Intervene, Lord, on our behalf, that brutality may cease and that all people may know peace.

Leader: Grant, all-powerful God, that your Holy Spirit may enlighten us at every moment so that we may be aware of the dangers that threaten our environment, our brothers and sisters, and ourselves. By your great mercy, may we be delivered from hardness of heart, that in all our actions we may proclaim your glory. We ask this through the precious blood of Jesus Christ, our sole mediator and advocate with you.

All: Amen.

BIBLE READING
Jeremiah 1:4–10

Leader: The message that God asks Jeremiah to give is difficult. Conditions are disastrous and Jeremiah is to speak the truth without losing hope for survival.

We can focus on the urgency of God's call in scripture and in our own lives, and the urgency of the call for help from those who are in need, by hearing about a Haitian expression: 'Anm'wé' *[pronounced An way]*. 'Anm'wé' is a call of alarm, widely used by the people of Haiti. The word cannot be translated but it is immediately understood when it is used. When someone hears 'Anm'wé', they must respond. They cannot be indifferent. The hearer must look, see and act.

For example, a truck had been parked on a hill when its brakes gave out. The truck began to roll down the hill toward people's yards, indeed towards people's poor makeshift houses. Everyone who saw what was happening called out 'Anm'wé'. Because of this call, people were alerted to danger and were able to respond by getting out of the way, or by helping others, or by seeing what they could do.

Woman 1: *(Shouting loudly)* 'Anm'wé!'

All: 'Anm'wé! Anm'wé!'

Woman 1: 'Anm'wé!' Let my cry come to our Father who is in heaven, so that in his mercy the people of Haiti may find grace in his sight. We know the word of God, we believe that this word is truth, but today we are caught up in a whirlwind, not knowing which direction to take. The people are in anguish, confused in the midst of the behaviour of those who defy the law and act corruptly.

All: Spirit of the living God, help the people of Haiti to recognize, among the many voices which come at them, your voice asking them to keep your word and to love their neighbours as themselves.

Woman 2: *(Shouting loudly)* 'Anm'wé!'

All: 'Anm'wé! Anm'wé!'

Woman 2: 'Anm'wé!' Our country stands on the brink. We invite you to join us in praying to the Lord that he will change the situation in which we have been living for several years. We grieve that our children are victims of hunger, injustice and oppression. They are cut down from their earliest years because they dare to claim their most fundamental rights.

All: We lift our hands to heaven to implore God's grace on Haiti, so that it may be freed from the evils that beset it.

Woman 3: *(Shouting loudly):* 'Anm'wé!'

All: 'Anm'wé! Anm'wé!'

Woman 3: 'Anm'wé!' Help, my friends, come and join us. Let us weep and cry to God, for many sufferings are the lot of his children in this world. They come in different forms —sexism, violence and immorality, prostitution, drugs, war, poverty, homelessness, injustice and insecurity, abuses of all kinds. Some of these evils have been inflicted on us by others, while we ourselves are responsible for a good number of them. My pain and suffering are also yours, sisters and brothers in Christ.

All: O God our Father, touch the hearts of those who inflict such pain and suffering, so that they may respond favourably to your call of love. Grant us to understand our responsibility towards others so as to lessen suffering among our brothers and sisters.

Woman 4: *(Shouting loudly)* 'Anm'wé!'

All: 'Anm'wé! Anm'wé!'

Woman 4: 'Anm'wé!' We are hungry and thirsty, our homeless sleep on the streets, our children look for food in rubbish piles. They are sick, with no hope of being healed, for want of medical care and adequate hospitals. Our immediate surrounds are filth and stench. These living conditions bring us a sense of frustration and shame. But in spite of all, I believe in Jesus Christ who delivers and saves. We know that God our Father will not abandon us, because we are his children. Brothers and sisters, our pain is immense. Help, help us! *[Pause]* Christians of the entire world, let us unite in prayer.

Silence.

ANTIPHONAL READING: PSALM 27

A: The Lord is my light and my salvation; I will fear no one.

B: The Lord protects me from all danger; I will never be afraid.

A: When evil men attack me and try to kill me, they stumble and fall.

B: Even if a whole army surrounds me, I will not be afraid.

A: Even if enemies attack me, I will still trust God.

B: I have asked the Lord for one thing; one thing only do I want:

A: To live in the Lord's house all my life, to marvel there at his goodness, and to ask for his guidance.

B: In times of trouble he will shelter me; he will keep me safe in his temple and make me secure on a high rock.

A: So I will triumph over my enemies around me. With shouts of joy I will offer sacrifices in his temple; I will sing, I will praise the Lord.

B: Hear me, Lord, when I call to you! Be merciful and answer me!

A: When you said, 'Come and worship me,' I answered, 'I will come, Lord; don't hide yourself from me!'

B: Don't be angry with me; don't turn your servant away.

A: You have been my help; don't leave me, don't abandon me, O God, my saviour.

B: My father and mother may abandon me, but the Lord will take care of me.

A: Teach me, Lord, what you want me to do, and lead me along a safe path, because I have many enemies.

B: Don't abandon me to my enemies, who attack me with lies and threats.

A: I know that I will live to see the Lord's goodness in this present life.

B: Trust in the Lord. Have faith, do not despair.

All: Trust in the Lord.

Leader: When we reflect on the reading from Jeremiah, we see that God touched Jeremiah's mouth, empowering him to speak as a prophet to his people. As we read about the call to Mary, we will see how she was reassured. God's power and love are manifested both in the call and in the response.

BIBLE READING
Luke 1:26–38

Leader: As God called Jeremiah and Mary and empowered them to do his will, so he calls each one of us to express his love and concern for all his world. And when he calls we must respond.

PRAYERS OF INTERCESSION

Leader: Let us pray for the people of Haiti and their country. Lord, you have made us guardians of your creation. Show us how we can work in partnership with the people of Haiti to help revitalize their environment, so enabling them to produce sufficient food for their needs.

All: Lord, hear our prayer.

Leader: All authority comes from you, Lord. Give the leaders of Haiti the vision to make wise decisions for the common good.

All: Lord, hear our prayer.

Leader: We pray for the women of Haiti. May your Holy Spirit enliven them and make them able to change structures in their local communities. May they participate actively in every form of peaceful struggle to establish justice and peace. May they encourage their children to know you and respond to your urgent call of love.

All: Lord, hear our prayer.

Silence.

VOICE FROM HAITI

All: God, our guide, we live in hope for the future:
we are determined to go on,
to venture with the help of our partners,
making great effort,
so that 'those who were no people'

may truly become your people.
Difficult days lie ahead,
but we believe that in the end,
with your help,
we shall overcome.

Leader: The women of Haiti are one with people in many parts of the world who are suffering in dire conditions. Thinking of all who are suffering, we need to pray for a deeper realization that when God calls us he will empower those who respond. 'I alone know the plans I have for you, plans to bring you prosperity and not disaster, plans to bring about the future you hope for.' *(Jeremiah 29:11, GNB)*

Today may our ears be open to hear and our hearts ready to carry out God's plan for the well-being of the whole human community.

God calls you—Answer! Every day God tells you, 'Come! This is the hour for you to respond.'

BLESSING

All: Lord, lead us from darkness into light,
From falsehood into truth,
From fear to trust.
Lead us from hatred into love,
From war to peace.
May peace fill our hearts, our world and the whole of creation.
Amen.

4

LIKE A SEED WHICH
GROWS INTO A TREE

Korea

BACKGROUND

Korea's location, close to China and Japan, has been the dominant influence in its cultural heritage. It has been open to attack from both of these countries. From 1910 to 1945, it was occupied by Japan. Then, at the end of World War II, the country was partitioned, with a Communist regime in the north and American-enforced government in the south. North Korea invaded the south in 1950, a conflict that continued until 1953. It was resolved in a ceasefire that divided the country on the 38th Parallel. This division weighs heavily with the people of the south. One aspect of the division is the splitting of families. Limited access across the demilitarized zone in 1985 allowed some families to meet for the first time in 45 years.

Until the 1960s, the main industry in South Korea was agriculture. By the 1990s, as one of the export-orientated 'tiger economies', it saw rapid industrialization, although the regional financial crisis of 1997–99 had a negative impact on the country for a time. The years of economic growth have had a tremendous impact on the whole nation. Unemployment is low—around 3 per cent. However, a large part of national income is spent on defence, to the detriment, perhaps, of the people's welfare.

South Korea has religious freedom and a considerable spiritual awakening has been taking place. The capital, Seoul, has over 2000 churches and these are constantly growing. Some of them have the largest congregations in the world! Christians are active in evangelism and fervent in their prayers, especially for the reunification of their country and the reconciliation of north and south.

Despite all the advances made in their country, the women of South Korea still feel that there is discrimination against women and girls. They look forward to a time when they will have a new sense of personal worth and dignity. They hope that the seeds of prayer may grow into fruitful trees, whose leaves may offer the shade of love, peace and reconciliation for their country.

WELCOME

Leader 1: Greetings from South Korean Christian women: 'An Nyung Haseyo!' *[pronounced Ahn Yung Hasayo]*

In Korea, people greet one another by saying, 'An Nyung Haseyo', which is very similar in meaning to the Hebrew word *shalom* or 'peace'. It implies a peaceful state of being, free from worry and anxiety. Each morning, Korean people greet one another by asking if all has been well the previous night.

Leader 2: This greeting grew out of Korea's long history of 5000 years, when it was frequently invaded by stronger neighbouring countries.

In spite of this, Korea was one country with one history, one language, one culture and one people until the end of World War II. People then looked forward to independence and a bright and happy future. However, outside powers divided the country into two parts with very different political systems. This led to the Korean

War. Although the fighting stopped, there was no peace treaty and now there is no possibility of visits or other kinds of communication between north and south. There are ten million family members who still dream of meeting each other.

The women of South Korea fervently pray for the reunification of their country and that God's peace will bring about a real 'An Nyung' in Korea and everywhere else throughout the world.

All: 'An Nyung Haseyo.'

Stand and greet those around you with these words.

CALL TO WORSHIP

Leader 3: As we turn to the parables, we first take note that Jesus began his lessons on the kingdom of God with the command to listen. Let us strive to hear God's word and accept it, and thus bring forth abundant fruit. Let us renew our trust that when God's word takes root and grows, the true 'an nyung' and 'shalom' will rule the world. Let us pray that God's kingdom will come so that there will be peace in Korea and the world.

All of us who enter into this worship are newborn in Christ Jesus who died on the cross and was resurrected. So let us experience in this time of prayer and worship the lessons of the parables. Let us deepen our understanding of how seeds are affected by different soils. Let us marvel that the smallest seed will grow into a great tree. Let us pray that we will hear and understand the meaning of God's kingdom here and now.

BIBLE READING
Mark 4:26–32

PRAYER OF THE SEEDS

Leader 1: Let us pray.

A gong is struck for the first time—for Liberation.

Leader 1: Come, O God of Salvation.
Come to those all over the world who are crying out in pain, because they are suffering and adrift through injustice, loneliness and alienation.
O God, we ask you to bring forth in our lives and communities the new seeds for liberation.

Korean melody

Come, come Lord ___ Je-sus, Cre - a - tor of ___ Peace.

Help us to be - come one bo-dy here on ___ earth.

Response: Come, come Lord Jesus, Creator of Peace.
Help us to become one body here on earth.

The gong is struck for the second time—for the Restoration of Creation.

Leader 2: Come, O God who gives us new life.

The beautiful earth which you have given us is dying and the order of life is breaking down due to our greed and selfishness.

O God, we ask you to bring forth in our lives and communities the new seeds for restoration of life and re-creation.

Response: Come, come Lord Jesus, Creator of Peace.
Help us to become one body here on earth.

The gong is struck for the third time—for World Peace and Unity.

Leader 3: Come, O God who makes us one with your peace.

We have prayed for the pains and suffering of all humanity. Korean people have endured suffering under imperialism and oppression by the powerful. Because of the division of their country they have fought each other and terrible destruction has occurred. Incredible feelings of hatred have been felt towards those of the same nationality.

O God, we ask you to bring forth in our lives and communities the new seeds for world peace and unity.

Response: Come, come Lord Jesus, Creator of Peace.
Help us to become one body here on earth.

Silent prayer.

All: O God of liberation and the restoration of creation, O God of peace and unity, we offer our thanks to you

because your word is sown within us. We praise you
and glorify your name.

BIBLE READING
Mark 4:2–9

ENCOUNTER WITH LIVES

Leader 1: Some seeds fell on the hard path. For some Koreans this
was the road that divided North and South Korea. For
others it was the sorrows, suffering and death of the
'Comfort Women' drafted into sexual slavery in Japan.
When the path is hard, the seed cannot sprout.

Leader 2: Some seeds fell on stony ground, where the dignity
of women is ignored and they are considered of little
worth. This stony ground reveals that even in the
church, it is still difficult for men and women to be
equal partners. These seeds face too many obstacles to
grow. They are bruised, scarred and crushed.

Leader 1: Some seeds fell among thorn bushes, where people live
only for their own happiness and well-being, without
caring for their suffering neighbours. The seeds cannot
grow or bear any fruit because they are choked.

Leader 2: But some seeds fell into a rich soil, where they sprouted
and grew into strong, fruitful plants. Who will provide
such good and rich soil?

PRAYERS OF CONFESSION

Leader 3: Let us pray.

All: Loving God, we have sinned against you by taking the easy way and by not realizing the infinite potential you have given us. We have sinned against you by resisting any change. We did not take care of your seed, your word sown within us. God, forgive us.

Leader 3: Let us listen to the confessions of some of our Korean sisters.

Woman 1: *(Around her neck hangs the label 'Patriarchy'.)* I was one who took the easy way in a patriarchal society. I desired and sought only my family's well-being and happiness, without caring about others, not even whether they lived or died. I was just happy living in the shadow of others.

She lifts off the label of 'Patriarchy', tears it up and places it at the feet of Woman 3.

All: Lord, have mercy.

Woman 2: *(Around her neck hangs the label 'Women as commodities'.)* I am a woman who did not resist the system that sees women as beautiful commodities. I only sought a life of beauty and extravagance, but it was in vain, and now I only have ugly scars to show for it.

She lifts off the label 'Women as commodities', tears it up and places it at the feet of Woman 3.

All: Lord, have mercy.

Woman 3: *(Around her neck hangs the label 'Victim of sexual slavery'.)* I am a woman who has been crushed and downtrodden —a victim of sexual slavery.

Women 1 and 2 remove her label and put their arms around her.

Women 1 & 2: You have been crushed and downtrodden as a result of wars between nations and races. You have been abandoned by society. You were made to feel hopeless. You were robbed of your own sense of personal worth and dignity. Even though you have endured unbearable suffering, no one has apologized or sought your forgiveness. Even your own society forgot about you long ago.

All: Lord, have mercy.

THE WORD OF FORGIVENESS

Leader 1: The Lord says, 'Now, let's settle the matter. You are stained red with sin, but I will wash you as clean as snow.' *(Isaiah 1:18, GNB)*

Leader 2: But God has shown us how much he loves us—it was while we were still sinners that Christ died for us! By his sacrificial death we are now put right with God; how much more, then, will we be saved by him from God's anger! *(Romans 5:8–9, GNB)*

Women return to their places.

PRAYERS OF INTERCESSION

Leader 3: Plough new ground for yourselves, plant righteousness, and reap the blessings that your devotion to me will produce. It is time for you to turn to me, your Lord, and I will come and pour out blessings on you. (*Hosea 10:12, GNB*)

Voice 1: Let us pray for Korea.

> O God, source of all life,
> you promised that justice would flow like a river,
> that debts would be cancelled,
> slaves released and land restored.
> Forgive the sins which divide Korea,
> separating North from South,
> Korean from Korean.
> Govern the hearts and minds
> of those in authority,
> that your holy will of reconciliation,
> peace and unity,
> will come to Korea
> and to the whole world.

All: (*Remain seated/kneeling*)
> Peace is flowing like a river,
> Flowing out through you and me,
> Spreading out into the desert,
> Setting all the captives free.

Voice 2: Let us pray for the Church in the world.

> Lord, we pray for your Church in the world.
> We pray that your people will seek your will

and proclaim your truth
that Jesus Christ came into the world
to save sinners.
Help us to uproot pride and self-righteousness,
so that humility will grow.
In love may we serve one another
and so bring about a society
where all are respected as persons.

All: Love is flowing like a river,
Flowing out through you and me,
Spreading out into the desert,
Setting all the captives free.

Voice 3: Let us pray for…
those for whom life has no meaning or purpose,
those who are without work and those who are
overworked,
those who are lonely or lost, in the big cities or
strange lands,
those who are dismayed that their efforts bring so
little change.
Give us courage so to act and so to speak that hope
may abound.

All: Hope is flowing like a river,
Flowing out through you and me,
Spreading out into the desert,
Setting all the captives free.

Silence.

PRAYER OF THANKSGIVING AND DEDICATION

Leader 1: Merciful God, who has granted us liberation and freedom, your love is eternal. Accept our love as we live with your love.

All: God of righteousness, you purposely chose what the world considers weak in order to shame the powerful. We thank you that it is your will that unjust systems and discrimination should be transformed. Lord God, be with us as we strive to live compassionately with the weak.

Leader 2: Loving God, who brings justice and reconciliation on this earth, thank you for your power to break down walls that divide. Be with us as we walk in peace.

All: O God, who made us one in Christ, we praise your name. Dwell with all those who strive to endure suffering as the body of Christ.

Leader 3: Eternal God, who continually creates history, help us to be your partners in this work of new creation.

All: O God, who can help us realize peace on earth, we thank you for your peace within us. Make us your disciples as we seek to live in peace.

BLESSING

Leader 1: 'An Nyung Haseyo.' Peace be with you.

All: 'An Nyung Haseyo.' Peace be with you.

Leader 1: Let us pray:

> May the God whose love never changes, whose word never fails and whose power never falters, strengthen our faith, inspire our hope and deepen our love, now and for ever.

All: Amen.

5

WHO IS MY NEIGHBOUR?

Madagascar

BACKGROUND

Madagascar is the third largest island in the world, a little larger than France. It is in the Indian Ocean, 500 miles east of Africa. Dense green forests and rice-growing areas cover part of the island, but the more dramatic red bare earth rising from the sea gives Madagascar the name of the 'Great Red Island'. With a tropical climate, hot and wet in the east, hot and dry in the south and west, annual cyclones cause very serious damage to this mainly agricultural country, part of which is prone to droughts. The island's agricultural products include rice, sugar cane, vanilla, peppercorns, cloves and coffee. National Parks and protected areas preserve precious wood orchids, tortoises and lemurs, of which several species are unique to the island. All this, together with beautiful butterflies, makes the island rich in natural beauty.

The population, of approximately 12.5 million, includes Asians of Indonesian origin, and Africans. Together they bring a varied culture to a very poor country where health care is inadequate and where there are serious problems of overgrazing and deforestation. Although social and economic problems surround the life of the people, care within family and community life is a priority.

Some women in Malagasy society are in positions of leadership, while others struggle to establish themselves. There are women's organizations in the country, which strive to improve justice for all.

Significant Christian mission started about 1820. Many Christians were persecuted in the reign of Queen Ranavalona. Among them was a woman named Rasaloma, who became the first martyr there. Now 55 per cent of the Malagasy people are Christian, with a wide variety of denominational loyalty. Many of the churches work to promote education and health in the towns and rural communities. Even though many people have become Christian, they have not necessarily rejected their native beliefs, which include ancestor worship.

Madagascar has had a stormy political history—first a kingdom, then a French protectorate and later a French colony. From 1958 the country became self-governing and then an independent republic. In 1992–93, free presidential and National Assembly elections took place, bringing to an end 17 years of simgle-party rule.

WELCOME

Leader 1: The women of Madagascar invite their sisters and brothers around the world to join with them in prayer. Let us unite in heart and spirit and worship Christ the Lord, for it is sweet to praise him and he is worthy of our adoration.

Madagascar is an island in the Indian Ocean and the people are rather isolated. There are several tribes of Malagasy, all speaking one common, living language. The island is rich in natural resources and attracts many visitors from all over the world, yet the people face many problems and difficulties.

Human relations are very important to them, and they have a special word, Fihavanana *[pronounced Fee-hav-a-na-na]* to describe the bond between people in all relationships, extending wider than parents, sisters, brothers and immediate relatives, across time and space.

CALL TO WORSHIP

Leader 2: Christ loves us and saves us. We can put our hope in him. His love is wonderful. So we invite our friends and neighbours throughout the world to join with us. 'Though we are many, we are one body in union with Christ, and we are all joined to each other as different parts of one body.' *(Romans 12:5, GNB)* Let us pray.

All: Lord, you are our God.
We call to you. Be with us.
In your presence we have courage.
Help us to know your love.
Lead us to praise and honour your glorious name.
May all who are thankful for your salvation say,
'How great is God!'
To God be the glory for ever. Amen.

Leader 2: O Lord our God, how great you are! You are clothed with majesty and glory. We praise you, O God our Father, for your wonderful love, which our human minds can barely grasp. You created us and sustain us. You are truly a God of love.

All: O loving and merciful God, we praise you.

Leader 2: We praise you, O God, for your love, which became flesh in Jesus Christ, your Son. Through him you have redeemed us and shown us how to love.

All: O loving and merciful God, we praise you.

Leader 2: We praise you, O God, for pouring out on us the gift of the Holy Spirit, who enables us to love not only in words but also in action.

All: O loving and merciful God, we praise you.

BIBLE READING
Luke 10:25–28

PRAYERS OF CONFESSION

Leader 1: O merciful and loving Father, you have commanded us to love our neighbours as ourselves, but we have sinned and disobeyed your laws.

All: O loving Lord, have mercy on us! We have not been good neighbours, and we ask you to forgive us.

Silent prayer.

Leader 1: Christ our Lord, we admit that we have not carried our neighbours' burdens. Selfishness still rules our lives. We are jealous and critical and quick to blame others.

All: O loving Lord, have mercy on us! We have not been good neighbours, and we ask you to forgive us.

Silent prayer.

Leader 1: O Holy Spirit, give us the grace to become good neighbours. Teach us what we should do.

All: Amen.

BIBLE READING
Luke 10:29–37

MALAGASY VOICES

Leader 2: We would like to share with you the experiences of people living in Madagascar, and of those who came to live among them, which show love in action. We thank God for the lives of those who showed mercy through acts of kindness and compassion.

Voice 1: In the southern part of Madagascar some years ago, a prolonged drought brought misery, starvation and famine. People had to sell everything they had to buy food and soon there was not even enough water to drink. Disease followed and people migrated for survival. This terrible famine reminds us of the experiences of the apostles: 'We go hungry and thirsty; we are clothed in rags… we wander from place to place.' (*1 Corinthians 4:11, GNB*)

Leader 2: In the time of Jesus, poverty, hunger, thirst and homelessness were well known. In many countries today there are similar situations. We pray that God will touch our hearts so that we can hear the cry of the poor and respond with love.

Voice 2: Hearing the voices of suffering, the Malagasy government organized an awareness campaign—SOS, Solidarity with the South—and the response from all sections of society was a readiness to help. As the Malagasy proverb says, 'The disaster that affects your relatives is also yours.' The people could not remain indifferent to their neighbours' need. Help also came to the remote island from individuals and organizations all around the world. Medical and feeding centres were set up, and for many months Christian volunteers gave their time and effort to help. As Paul says, 'Because of our love for you we were ready to share with you not only the Good News from God but even our own lives. You were so dear to us!' *(1 Thessalonians 2:8, GNB)*

Leader 2: We see an image of God's love in the faces of those who help others. We pray that God will strengthen the love in our hearts so that people will be willing to share what they have and the world will be transformed into a caring family.

Voice 3: There is still the fear in the south of Madagascar that the drought will recur and another disaster will strike this beautiful tourist area. The government has introduced schemes to conserve water, to provide food storage and to ensure the means of survival. It is a difficult and lengthy task and the people cannot do it alone. They need the help and support of friends all over the world who see the starving and thirsty people as neighbours indeed. As Jesus said, 'I assure you that anyone who gives you a drink of water because you belong to me will certainly receive his reward.' *(Mark 9:41, GNB)*

Leader 2: Let us pray.

O Holy Spirit, teach us to have a loving heart like Christ. Teach us to pray and act in love for each other. We pray that you will guide us. If we can show love for one another as Jesus taught us, then our whole world will be healed. We offer this prayer in the name of Jesus.

All: Amen.

COMMITMENT TO EACH OTHER

Leader 1: The Samaritan poured oil on the wounds of the man who was beaten and robbed. With this compassionate action we are shown how to answer the question, 'Who is my neighbour?' To show our desire to heal the wounds of the world, the divisions that separate people, let us touch one another with oil. *(See note on the passing of the oil, on page 68.)*

To strengthen our commitment to act with mercy and to show our compassion for one another, we will take the hand of the person beside us and say, 'I am your neighbour.'

All: I am your neighbour.

Leader 1: Let us pray.

All: O God, we have come together in prayer, knowing that you are present in our midst. We wish to know you better and worship you with joy. We offer ourselves to be your servants and to be good neighbours to one another. We trust in you with all our heart. We praise you for all you have done for us. We are happy that we are together in this worship service. We believe in the power of prayer and its ability to call everyone to fullness of life. Jesus, fill us with your love. We belong to you today, tomorrow and for ever. Amen.

Leader 1: Fihavanana is very important for Malagasy people. It is the bond that they have in all their relationships. Jesus understood and valued the relationships that we form in our families. He enlarged our understanding of family to include all who do the will of God.

BIBLE READING
Mark 3:31–35

PRAYERS OF INTERCESSION

Leader 2: Let us pray for all places in the world that are troubled by crises and violence.

O God, we pray for those places where violence and riots rob people of peace and security. We lift up cities made dangerous because of crimes that often end in murder. We pray for all people who have no peace and live in misery day and night. Deliver this world from violence and every kind of danger.

All: O God, you love us and in Jesus you show us how to love one another as neighbours. Hear our prayer.

Leader 1: Let us pray for all people who suffer from poverty.

O merciful God, you see those who are poor and have nobody to rely on. You know who is without shelter or food and who lives on the street. You hear their cry. Open our ears to hear their call, and our hearts to respond. Take away the greed in the world, so that all may learn to share what you have given.

All: O God, you love us and in Jesus you show us how to love one another as neighbours. Hear our prayer.

Leader 2: Let us pray for the healing of the earth.

Creator God, you know how people have defiled your gifts by the way they live and act. Restore our rivers, our air, our forests, our mountains and seas. Show us how to love all that you have made—how to take care of our environment and protect the beauty of your creation.

All: O God, you love us and in Jesus you show us how to love one another and to care for all creation. Hear our prayer.

Leader 1: Let us pray for leaders and ministers.

O God, all power and authority come from you. We ask your blessing for all those who govern. Fill our leaders with wisdom, justice and compassion. Bless also the ministers of our churches. Let your Holy Spirit guide and strengthen them, so that they may help us all to turn from selfishness and sin and become a people who love you and our neighbours.

All: O God, you love us and in Jesus you show us how to love one another as neighbours. Hear our prayer.

Leader 2: Let us pray for children and young people.

We know that some children have grown up in the church but have left the church behind. Lord, give them a deeper understanding of your truth. We pray for all families. Wherever there is pain and strife, pour out your love and healing. Wherever relationships have been broken, bring your peace and reconciliation.

All: O God, you love us and in Jesus you show us how to love one another as neighbours. Hear our prayer.

Leader 1: Let us pray for all women.

Women have an important role to play, yet many are denied equal opportunities in education and employment, and so fail to reach their full potential. Strengthen us to care for those around us, so that by your power we may help to make the world a better and more peaceful place.

All: O God, you love us and in Jesus you show us how to love one another. Hear our prayer.

Silence.

PRAYER OF THANKSGIVING AND DEDICATION

Leader 1: O God, we give thanks to you. How precious is your constant love for us. We thank you for the life and ministry of Jesus and for his death and resurrection. We praise you, God, and honour you for your holiness and love. Help us always to keep before us your commandment to love you and to love one another.

All: O Lord, thank you for calling us to be your people. Keep us in your love so that this communion of all Christians will not cease. Lord, take our love for each other as an honour given to you.

BLESSING

All: The grace of our Lord Jesus Christ, the love of God, the fellowship of the Holy Spirit, be with us now and evermore. Amen.

NOTE: PASSING OF THE OIL

On a table in front of or near to the leader will be small jars or pots of oil, placed there before the service (use olive oil or some sweet-smelling oil). Those appointed to pass round the oil will come forward. As Leader 1 says the words 'Touch one another with oil', she will touch the hand of the other leader with oil, and then the hand of each server, before they take the oil from person to person. The oil is returned to the table and the servers may remain at the front until the next Bible reading is announced. (The number of oil servers will depend on the number of people expected. An alternative is to use pads of cotton wool soaked in oil.)

6

GOD'S TENDER TOUCH

Venezuela

BACKGROUND

Venezuela is a South American country bordering the Caribbean Sea, with Columbia to the west and Brazil to the south and east. It is a country of contrasts, with beaches, rivers, forests and mountains. There are almost 30 million inhabitants, of whom 90 per cent live in urban areas. The capital is Caracas, and Spanish is the spoken language.

The country has many flowering plants and a great variety of trees. The national flower is an orchid. There is a variety of exotic birds, parrots, macaws and toucans, the latter being the national bird. Jaguars prowl deep in the jungle along with ocelots, deer, tapir, giant ant-eaters and many species of monkeys.

Christopher Columbus discovered Venezuela in 1498. He was followed by other Spanish explorers, who settled on the northern coasts of Venezuela. In the 1800s, Venezuelans began to fight for their freedom from Spain, and they became independent in 1821. They were led by Simon Bolivar (the currency is named after him). When oil wealth hit the country in the 1920s, agriculture was no longer important and there was a massive migration from the country to the cities.

World oil prices began to slide in 1982 and this caused much poverty in the country. Venezuelans still live with the memory of the oil boom years, which began with the nationalization of the oil industry and ended with a crash in 1983, which is now referred to as 'Black Friday'. The country is still very dependent on oil, and the price fluctuations in this industry remain an ongoing problem.

A population boom in the 1970s has led to Venezuela becoming overwhelmingly young. Today 67 per cent are under 30 years of age. The oil crash led to unemployment, which in turn led to the disintegration of the family, forcing women to assume the role of both parents to their usually numerous children. A significant percentage of the population remains below the poverty line.

The official religion is Catholicism, with only 10 per cent of the population being members of Protestant churches. Deep in the Amazonian forest, meanwhile, are Indian villages little affected by the march of time.

WELCOME

A large unlit candle is to be brought in and placed in an appropriate place in front of the congregation.

Leader: In Venezuela, when people meet, they greet each other by requesting and receiving a blessing. The formula is simple and beautiful and the Spanish is easy to pronounce. Please repeat after me:

'Bendicion' ('A blessing, please').
[Pronounced: Ben-dees-ee-on]

'Dios te bendiga' ('God bless you').
[Pronounced: Dios tay ben-dee-ga]

Practise two or three times till everyone is familiar with the words.

CALL TO WORSHIP

Leader: We invite you to begin this time of worship by turning to one another and greeting each other in the Venezuelan way.

All: 'Bendicion.'
'Dios te bendiga.'

Leader: Let us pray.

Dear loving, heavenly Father, how wonderful it is to be in your presence. We worship and adore you for who you are and what you mean to us. We thank you for your steadfast love, mercy and faithfulness. You are the giver of life and our sovereign Lord, and we offer you our sacrifice of praise. Amen.

A verse from scripture: 'Take delight in the Lord, and he will give you the desires of your heart. Commit your way to the Lord; trust in him, and he will act.' *(Psalm 37:4–5, NRSV)*

We now consider God's tender touch expressed in the blessings he gives to us.

PRAYERS OF THANKSGIVING

Leader: Let us listen to the prayers of thanksgiving from the women of Venezuela.

Voice 1: Our creator God, Lord of heaven and earth, who gives us each new day, we take delight in all the peoples of the earth and in all of your creation. So with our sisters and brothers in Venezuela and all round the world, we sing:

Response: (*Sung*) We give thanks unto the Lord, we give thanks. We give thanks unto the Lord.

Cesáreo Gabaráin

Voice 2: For our country, which has been blessed by your tender touch with so many natural riches, beautiful landscapes and wonderful weather…

Response: We give thanks unto the Lord… etc.

Voice 3: For your tender and protective touch on each person in our country who has become an unknown hero in the daily struggle to create a better Venezuela…

Response: We give thanks unto the Lord… etc.

Voice 4: For the cultural wealth visible in our rhythmic variety, musical talent and our colourful and physical expressiveness, all of which are signs of your tenderness…

Response: We give thanks unto the Lord… etc.

Voice 5: For your tender touch, which strengthens and sustains our sense of family, our ability to laugh even in the midst of sorrow, the smile of our children despite the violence, the determination of women in their constant struggle in the face of discrimination…

Response: We give thanks unto the Lord… etc.

Leader: Now let us give thanks for God's tender touch on our own country.

Voice 6: We thank you, Father, for this land; for mountains and green valleys; for farm land and the seaside; for city street and village green; and we praise you for the changing seasons. For your tender touch on our children, the elderly, those who are willing to care for their neighbours and on those whom we love and those who love us…

Response: We give thanks unto the Lord… etc.

Leaders: We now consider God's tender touch expressed in forgiveness.

BIBLE READING
Hosea 11:1–3

PRAYERS OF CONFESSION

Leader: Let us listen to the prayers of the women of Venezuela.

Voice 7: We confess that we have distanced ourselves from you, Lord, when we didn't hear your call in the mute cry of desperate people in our country who suffer from all forms of violence.

Silent prayer.

Voice 8: We as a church confess that we have often created new false gods and new idols, which distract us from you.

Silent prayer.

Leader: Just as the women of Venezuela have confessed their sins, we too must make confession of the sins of our nation.

Silent prayer.

Leader: Let us pray together.

All: We come before you today, O God, all of us together, just as we are. We ask forgiveness because we have failed when we stopped doing good, when we abandoned the sick and the suffering. For our sins and failures we cry out for forgiveness.

BIBLE READING

Hosea 11:4 (first time)

Leader: Put down your service sheets and hold the hands of the people on your left and right.

Let us feel the strength of the person beside us. Let us feel the human warmth.

Let us feel the skin and physical touch. We will listen again to this reading from Hosea.

BIBLE READING

Hosea 11:4 (second time)

Leader: Now we will listen to the promise of God as it is written in verse 9: 'I am the Holy One in your midst.'

God is calling us to follow him and to do his will. God wishes to touch us and unite us with love. God does not want to abandon us at all, even if we are rebellious. God wishes to give us his blessing.

Let go your hands and turn to the person beside you and share his or her blessing as we did in the beginning:

All: 'Bendicion.'

'Dios te bendiga.'

Leader: We now consider God's tender touch expressed in his response to our petitions.

BIBLE READING
Luke 8:43–48

PRAYERS OF INTERCESSION

A woman walks to the front and puts on a cloak which has pinned on to it large strips of cloth or paper bearing the words Teenage Pregnancy, Violence, Unemployment & Homelessness, Malnutrition, and one word that you have chosen to add on behalf of your own community. (See note on page 80.)

A young teenager comes up, removes the strip with the words Teenage Pregnancy, holds it up and reads it aloud. She then places the strip next to the large candle and speaks to everyone.

Woman 1: I am 15 years old and I want to share with you a concern I have. Twenty per cent of the pregnant women of Venezuela are under the age of 19. Most are my age! The number of teenage mothers and the mortality rate as a result of self-induced abortions is very high. Please pray for us so that we can overcome ignorance and succeed in our struggle against sexual violence.

Silent prayer.

A poorly dressed woman comes up and removes the word Violence, holds it up and reads it aloud. She then places the strip next to the large candle and speaks to everyone.

Woman 2: Can there be a greater violence than the one produced by poverty? I ask you to pray for those living under conditions of poverty. I ask you to pray especially for women, who carry the greatest burden in this situation and who are constantly exposed to violence.

Silent prayer.

A woman comes up and removes the words Unemployment & Homelessness, holds it up and reads it aloud. She then places the strip next to the large candle and speaks to everyone.

Woman 3: I am Clara. I have lost my job, like many others in Venezuela. We are living in a time of economic crisis, which makes it difficult to find work. I am using up my savings in order to buy food for us to eat.

We run the risk of losing our house because we can't afford to pay for it. I ask you to pray for all of us who are anguished because we want to work and to live.

Silent prayer.

A woman comes up and removes the word Malnutrition, holds it up and reads it aloud. She then places the strip next to the large candle and speaks to everyone.

Woman 4: Our children are the main victims of the economic crisis. They do not have sufficient food. Every day more children become malnourished and die of disease. They continue suffering abuse and they don't have the opportunity to study. Please pray for them.

Silent prayer.

A local woman comes up and removes the word for your own community, holds it up and reads the word aloud. She then places the strip next to the large candle and speaks to everyone.

77

Woman 5: *[Prayers of Intercession are said for the local community. See note on page 80.]*

Silent prayer.

The woman who has been wearing the cloak lights the candle and then speaks.

Woman 6: As light breaks the darkness, so the presence of God lights the darkness that surrounds so many people.

Leader: Let us pray.

Lord, protect with the power of your Spirit and your love all those who suffer from injustice; those who are tortured, raped and persecuted.

Protect the children who are abused, who are hungry and have no possibility of going to school.

Help us to see when our neighbour suffers any form of discrimination.

Give us the courage to overcome fear and cowardice. Give us the wisdom and the will to commit ourselves to struggle for justice for and with others.

Lord, send your Holy Spirit to world leaders so that violence and corruption may be replaced by love. Amen.

BIBLE READING
Mark 10:13–16

Voice 9: Sisters and brothers, we want the situation in our country to change. This can only happen when our fellow citizens and especially our government grow closer to Jesus and receive his tender touch like children, in total surrender, complete trust, absolute belief and humility without the desire for power. Let us assume the responsibility for bringing ourselves to Jesus. In the land of Venezuela we need your support and partnership in prayer.

PRAYERS OF THANKSGIVING AND DEDICATION

Leader: Let us pray.

All: We thank you, God,
that your tender touch strengthens our faith,
gives us unlimited confidence,
prepares us for love;
opens our path to the weak and abused,
opens our senses to perceive where there is brutality,
dehumanization, all forms of violence;
prepares for passive resistance against violence,
teaches us to see with our hearts,
prepares us to believe like children
and makes the seed germinate,
so that the message of the gospel can be reborn in
each one of us.

Leader: Our Lord, we praise you and are grateful to you. You are with us in the darkness of this world and give us the strength to remain with you. You take us from the darkness to the light with your tender touch.

All: Lord, touch our eyes that we may see,
touch our ears that we may hear,
touch our mouths that we may transmit your message,
touch our hands that they may be willing to give,

touch our lives, so that your Holy Spirit may
penetrate them,
touch our hearts and let us feel your love.

BLESSING

Leader: Let us end our worship by turning to the person beside
us and giving each other the blessing.

All: 'Bendicion.'
'Dios te bendiga.'

Leader: May God bless us and keep us.

All: Amen.

NOTE: PRAYERS OF INTERCESSION

Prepare a statement and prayer request for your own community,
along the lines of the ones from Venezuela. Use this at the point
indicated during the prayers of intercession.

7

TALITHA KOUM:
YOUNG WOMAN, STAND UP

Indonesia

BACKGROUND

The 17,500 islands of Indonesia form the world's largest archipelago, with a population of 220,000,000. It stretches some 5000 kilometres along the equator, through three time zones, separating the Indian and Pacific Oceans. The climate is tropical—hot, wet and humid.

The islands have many active volcanoes. Though potentially dangerous, they do help to enrich the soil, which supports lush vegetation with many exotic flowers, birds and animals. Much of the tropical forest, which formerly covered wide areas, has been destroyed, causing soil erosion. The main food crop is rice. Many types of fruit and spices are exported, as well as timber. Oil and gas are extracted from the sea.

Traditional crafts are important throughout the islands, making use of materials ranging from precious stones to palm leaves. Most famous are the Ikat weaving and the Batik dyeing.

Formerly known as the Spice Islands, Indonesia was for 350 years a Dutch colony. Independence was finally gained in 1947, when Sukarno became President of the new Republic of Indonesia. He was succeeded in 1968 by Suharto, and President Habibie took office in 1998, followed by President Wahid in 1999 and President Megawati in 2001. The political situation remains volatile. Students have been to the fore in the struggle for greater democracy.

Economically, the country has suffered in recent years, not only because of the financial crisis in south-east Asia in the mid to late 1990s but also from the drought brought about by El Nino in 1997–98. This led to forest fires, which destroyed crops, ruined land and caused widespread pollution. Many people live below the poverty line, and the sheer size of Indonesia creates severe economic problems.

Women have always been treated as inferior to men in Indonesia. They have been taught to keep silent. The situation is slowly improving, however.

WELCOME

A gong or a bell is struck three times to signal that the time of worship is about to start.

Leader: You will have seen or heard about the beautiful islands of Indonesia, but in recent times the people have been suffering from extreme economic problems, droughts, devastating fires and pollution. Political changes have been made and difficult situations have had to be faced—but the women of Indonesia have not lost faith. They lead us to focus on Jairus and his daughter and point us to their hope for the future, that young people will carry our faith into the years to come.

We celebrate with renewed conviction and commitment that Jesus came into the world to bring new life.

A gong or a bell is again struck three times.

DRAMATIC PROCESSION (SEE NOTE ON PAGE 91)

While sorrowful music is played, someone representing a girl of 12, and a group of women, process in. Each woman shows one of the realities that many women in the world experience. The girl lies down in front of the congregation, appearing to be ill or even dead.

The Leader goes to the girl, lifts up her hand and speaks.

Leader: Talitha koum; little girl, I tell you to get up!

The mood changes. Lively music plays as the girl stands up. The women lay down their burdens and help to liberate one another. Their burdens, chains and gags are left behind as they join the congregation. The girl takes a posy of spring flowers, symbolizing new life and resurrection, turns to the congregation and joyfully gives her testimony.

CALL TO WORSHIP

Young girl: I am alive. Yes! I am alive and well! Jesus has raised me up and given me life.

All women of Indonesia unite!

All men of Indonesia unite!

All children of Indonesia unite!

Come, you Christian people all over the world.

Come, you who are chained and oppressed.

Come, you who are helpless and harassed.

Come, you who are marginalized and you who are suffering.

My sisters in faith, arise!

My brothers in faith, arise!

Let us come to the Lord, the giver of life!

The girl lights the candle and returns to the congregation.

Leader: Let us stand and say together…

All: *(Standing)* Lord God, you are the source of life, the Lord of resurrection. Here we are, O Lord, we humbly come to you.

Leader: The power of God the Father sustains our life
and inspires us to live in the fullness of life.
The love of Jesus Christ lifts our hearts and gives us joy.
The Spirit liberates us from our differences
so that we may live in unity.

PRAYER OF THANKSGIVING

Leader: Let us pray.

Living God and source of all life,
we thank you for your warm touch,
that opens our eyes and our hearts to see your glory.
We thank you for your wonderful help,
that strengthens our faith and gives us courage.
We thank you for your gentle calling,
that warms our hearts and fills us with love.
Let each one of us enter into a new life with joy,
a life that overflows with hope because of your power.

All: Amen.

PRAYERS OF CONFESSION

Leader: O Lord God, you are the giver of life who unites us in the bond of love and calls us to live in harmony.

Voice 1: In your presence we confess that in our family life we do not always listen to and support one another. We seek to control rather than to serve each other.

Family life has lost its togetherness and its unity. We have not always lived in harmony with one another.

In many countries there are barriers which prevent people realizing their full potential. We confess that we have allowed this to narrow our horizons, and self-doubt has prevented us from taking action.

We have allowed ourselves to be conditioned to sacrifice our lives as a duty and so failed to enjoy them as gifts from you.

Silent prayer.

Leader: O Lord God, you are the head of the Church. You call on us, your people, to grow together.

Voice 2: In your presence we confess that we, your people, have thought only of our own narrow self-interests, denying others a share of your kingdom.

We have not overcome those structures that perpetuate inequality.

We have allowed the gulf between generations to continue.

We have not always recognized the presence of God in others.

Though we are your servants, we have lost our confidence and our spirit; we have become discouraged and feel helpless.

We have not shown the unity of the body of Christ in your Church.

Silent prayer.

Leader: O God, ruler of the universe, you always plan good things for all your creation.

Voice 3: In your presence we confess that we have not been willing to share;
   instead we have become greedy.
We have not loved each other;
   instead we have oppressed one another.
We have not appreciated others;
   instead we have looked down on them.
We have not maintained our environment;
   instead we have destroyed it.

Silent prayer.

RENEWAL OF LIFE

Leader: In this third millennium, we still carry old problems. We even carry the debts of our parents. We also face the confusion and complexity of advanced technology. We struggle against those business practices that crush the lives of workers and destroy our forests and oceans. But we are not without hope. We are not without power.

Christ died for us and rose from the dead.

All: In Christ we are forgiven.

Leader: Christ died for us and rose from the dead.

All: In Christ we have abundant life.

Leader: Christ died for us and rose from the dead.

All: Jesus Christ is the same yesterday, today and for ever.

Leader: In our reading from Paul's second letter to Timothy, we are reminded that young Christians need encouragement.

BIBLE READING
2 Timothy 1:5–14

Young woman: As young people, we are concerned about the many ethical issues in our lives. We are overwhelmed by social problems and are losing our identity.

Leader: As Paul wrote to Timothy...

All: I remind you to fan into flame the gift of God, which is in you... For God did not give us a spirit of timidity, but a spirit of power, of love and of self-discipline *[NIV]*.

Leader: It is our challenge, our concern and responsibility as the Church to prepare and strengthen one another, to enable us to respond to the changes in our time and to bear witness to God's power, the power of resurrection!

All: I remind you to fan into flame the gift of God, which is in you... For God did not give us a spirit of timidity, but a spirit of power, of love and of self-discipline.

Young woman: Let our enthusiasm for learning and a willingness to work hard grow within us. Let us strengthen our spiritual life so that we can choose good rather than evil. Let us increase our persistence and courage.

In a symbolic gesture of care, I invite you all to help each other to stand up.

Leader: *(Waiting until everyone is standing)* Let us again say to one another these words from Paul's second letter to Timothy.

All: I remind you to fan into flame the gift of God, which is in you… For God did not give us a spirit of timidity, but a spirit of power, of love and of self-discipline.

PRAYERS OF INTERCESSION

Leader: Let us pray for the troubles of the world.

We pray for those in the world who have forgotten that all people are made in your image and likeness and are of equal worth in your eyes;

for those who suffer because of racial oppression and social injustice;

for those who struggle for human dignity;

for those who have lost their hope for the future.

We pray for the needy and suffering in the world;

for the hungry and thirsty;

for the homeless;

for the unemployed and unemployable;

for the victims of alcoholism;

for the victims of drug addiction;

for the sick, in mind or body;

for the lonely and elderly.

We pray for all parents, that they may give their children the love and guidance which will help them to find the right way in life;

for all children without parents;

for young people, that they may find hope for the future;

for peace between nations and goodwill among all people;

Lord, hear us!

WRITTEN BY THE WORLD DAY OF PRAYER COMMITTEE OF SWEDEN IN 1984

All: Lord, graciously hear us.

Silent prayer.

Leader: Lord, hear us.

All: Lord, graciously hear us.

BIBLE READING
Mark 5:21–24, 35–43

JOINT DECLARATION

Young woman: As young women of Indonesia, we have a vision for the future, while at the same time we are facing discrimination because of our youth. Lack of experience and opportunity to study have become obstacles that prevent us from taking our full part in church and society.

All: With God, our source of hope, we promise to support young people.

Refrain: *(Sung)* Talitha koum, little girl, I tell you to get up!

Ta - lith - a   Koum   lit - tle____

girl   I tell you to get____ up.

Woman: As women of Indonesia, we have a vision of a new life of equality and of justice! We hold on to our vision even when society does not recognize our potential.

All: With God, our source of justice, we promise to support all women in their call for justice and mercy.

Refrain: Talitha koum, little girl, I tell you to get up!

Elderly woman: As elderly women of Indonesia, we have a vision of a better and more prosperous life, but we worry about the changing attitudes and behaviour that sweep away traditional values.

All: With God, our source of wisdom, may we be wiser in our actions and enabled to handle the problems that face us.

COMMISSIONING AND BLESSING

Leader: Rise up! You are alive because of the power of resurrection. Do not be afraid; only believe!

All stand.

All: Talitha koum; little girl, I tell you to get up!

Leader: Go therefore in the power of Jesus' resurrection. Proclaim to the world that his love is liberating and gives life.

All: Talitha koum, God bless you. Amen.

NOTE: DRAMATIC PROCESSION

As sorrowful music is played, a twelve-year-old girl (or someone representing a twelve-year-old girl) walks in as though she is very weak. Beside her walk two women, one carrying a small posy of spring flowers, the other carrying an unlit candle. They watch the girl as they walk, anxiety and sadness on their faces.

Behind this trio come women representing the various difficulties that women around the world suffer. Their faces and bearing should reflect the sadness and pain in their lives. This procession can contain as many or as few women as is practical in your local situation. There are many imaginative ways of representing the plight of the women, so be creative!

Some suggestions for their appearance might be:

- two with their mouths gagged
- two with their hands chained
- one carrying a baby (or doll) and perhaps dragging along another child
- one or two carrying 'heavy' loads on their backs
- a sensuously dressed woman wearing heavy make-up

When the girl lies down at the front, those who walk beside her place the candle and the posy on a table and join the other women as they spread out across the front, facing the girl, but not obstructing her from the congregation's view. Meanwhile, the worship leader speaks to the girl and she stands up.

As the lively music is played, the women lay down their burdens and help to unchain/ungag one another.

The one with the baby/doll could be supported by others, or someone could carry the baby/doll for her. The prostitute could put on some form of clothing to tone down her appearance. Again, be creative! The purpose is to show the women freed from whatever has burdened them and, with happy faces, joining the congregation.

The girl picks up the flowers, faces the congregation and gives her testimony (see order of service). Then she lights the candle before joining the congregation.

8

INFORMED PRAYER,
PRAYERFUL ACTION

Samoa

BACKGROUND

The islands of Samoa are found in the Pacific Ocean and form one of the smallest countries in the world—slightly larger than Luxembourg. Samoa is made up of two main islands, Savai'i and Upolu, and eight smaller ones, not all of which are inhabited.

The islands are volcanic in origin; the last eruption was in 1911. Coral reefs surround much of the coastline. The interiors are mountainous with dense tropical rainforest. There is little level land except in coastal areas, where most cultivation takes place. The climate is hot and rainy from November to April and cooler and drier from May to October. Samoa is prone to cyclones and hurricanes, which can cause great devastation. The environment is being put under pressure by efforts to increase revenue.

Samoans live simply, and life centres around the family. Many people live in extended family groups called *aiga*, led by a Matai. The Matai is responsible for the economic, social and political affairs of the family. Samoan women play an essential role in the family, village community, government and the church.

Religion is one of the most important aspects of Samoan culture and is incorporated in the islands' motto, 'Samoa is founded on God'.

About 99 per cent of Samoans are Christian. According to legend, it was prophesied that a new religion would come to Samoa. The arrival in 1830 of the Revd John Williams, of the London Missionary Society, was understood to be the fulfilment of the prophecy. He was accompanied by Samoans from Tahiti who helped him with his mission. A woman offered the first prayer spoken on Samoan soil. Acceptance of Christianity brought peace to the islands and is an example of how informed prayer develops into prayerful action.

Samoa is one of the world's least developed nations. Its economy has declined since independence in 1962. There is little industry. Coffee, groundnuts, bananas, yams and tropical fruit are grown mainly for local markets, with cash crops like coconut and cocoa grown for export. There has been a growth in the service sector with the development of offshore banking and tourism. Many Samoans live and work outside Samoa. Samoa is politically stable and believed to have one of the lowest crime rates in the world.

WELCOME

Leader: The women of Samoa welcome their sisters and brothers all over the world to join with them in prayer.

CALL TO WORSHIP

Leader: Those who trust in the Lord are like Mount Zion, which cannot be moved, but abides forever. *(Psalm 125:12, NRSV)*

All: I was glad when they said to me, 'Let us go to the house of the Lord!' *(Psalm 122:1, NRSV)*

Leader: Praise and glory be unto our loving God for ever. Come, let us worship our God who created us.

All: God our Creator, you are the source of life.
Merciful and loving God, you are the strength for
those who are weak.
You are the fount of all blessing.
You are the light in the darkness.
We call for the inspiration of the Holy Spirit, so that
we may be able to worship you in truth.
Creator of life, hear our prayer. Amen.

Leader: We welcome you to Samoa in the Pacific Ocean. Samoa
comprises two main islands and eight smaller ones.
Its motto is 'Samoa is founded on God'. Sunday
observance is crucial and everyone goes to church. The
Samoans are among the friendliest people in the world.
They still live in traditional villages and retain many of
the customs and traditions of their ancestors from
centuries ago.

KAVA CEREMONY (SEE NOTE ON PAGE 102)

Narrator: In Samoa, the Kava Ceremony has always been of deep
significance, full of life and at the heart of their culture.
It portrays some of the loveliest elements of the Samoan
character.

The Kava Ceremony is a special reception offered to
guests and friends. It is the expression of friendship and
the love that the Samoan people want to share with
their visitors.

When visitors arrive in the islands, arrangements are
immediately made for a Kava Ceremony. The chiefs
and orators meet at a place of welcome, bringing in kava
roots, their treasured possessions, from which a cere-
monial drink is prepared.

The ceremony has two orators—one who speaks on

behalf of the hosts, and one who responds on behalf of the guests.

Host orator: We present you the kava roots. They are our proof that you, our guests, have been accepted and received as friends and, even more, as sisters and brothers. With this symbol, we welcome you all in the name of our Lord Jesus Christ. As we come together, we are united in our Kava Ceremony.

Let us pray.

Lord, we thank you that you have brought us together. We pray that our guests, their families and friends may know the abundance of your love, the wonder of your peace and joy in all circumstances. Amen.

Narrator: The kava roots have been crushed to a powder and mixed with water. The chief gives a bowl of this to the guests, who pass it from hand to hand, each pouring out a few drops and saying the blessing, 'Ia Manuia'.

Guest orator: On behalf of the guests, I thank you for your warm welcome and prayers. We feel blessed by your friendship and love.

Let us pray.

Lord, we thank you that you have brought us together. We pray for the people of Samoa, who can teach us true welcome from the culture and traditions of their country. We pray that they will continue to seek your guidance, and experience your love and peace in their lives. Amen.

Narrator: In the Kava Ceremony, not only have we learnt about one another, but we have also entered into one another's lives. We have come to understand one another and we have prayed together. We will continue to pray together. Thus we can now draw on God's wisdom and see how we can act together on behalf of the whole community.

PRAYERS OF THANKSGIVING

Voice 1: Omnipotent and all-powerful God, we magnify your greatness. We praise your holy name. We thank you for the beauty and abundance to be found in creation, for the natural wonders to be found in Samoa and in each country of the world, and for our shared Christian heritage.

Response: *(Sung)* We give you thanks, our gracious Lord, we praise your holy name.

Samoan melody

We give you thanks our grac-ious Lord, we praise your ho-ly name.

Voice 1: We thank you for the word of God that brought us the knowledge of the saving grace of Jesus Christ, who died on the cross and rose from the dead for our redemption. We praise you for men and women who dedicated their lives to taking the gospel to different parts of the world.

Response: We give you thanks, our gracious Lord.
We praise your holy name.

Voice 2: God of inspiration, we thank you for the many ways women serve you and for the talents and gifts you have given us for the good of our world. We thank you for the enabling power of the Holy Spirit, which makes it possible for us to serve you better.

Response: We give you thanks, our gracious Lord.
We praise your holy name.

Voice 2: God of all time, we thank you for your faithfulness from the beginning of time and through every age. We know you are faithful and we are confident you will continue to guide the people of Samoa and all the nations of the world.

Response: We give you thanks, our gracious Lord.
We praise your holy name.

BIBLE READING
Esther 4:1–17

PRAYERS OF CONFESSION

Leader: 'Sa' is the Samoan word for 'sacred'. 'Sa' is also the nightly devotional time of prayer that is taken very seriously in Samoa. As darkness draws near, around 6.15pm, a village gong sounds or there is a conch call, signifying that the village should prepare for 'Sa'. When the second gong sounds, families begin to pray together. Fifteen minutes later, a third gong sounds to end 'Sa'.

Let us offer our prayers of confession:

God of compassion, we confess those times when we lacked faith and self-discipline and did not turn to you in prayer.

All: Lord, forgive us.

Silent prayer.

Leader: God of mercy, we confess those times when our selfishness caused disharmony and lack of understanding in our families and our communities.

All: Lord, forgive us.

Silent prayer.

Leader: Loving God, forgive us for the times when we have failed to see and respond to the hardship and suffering of children everywhere.

All: Lord, forgive us.

Silent prayer.

Leader: Lord, forgive us for failing to use and develop your gifts in ourselves and others.

All: Lord, forgive us.

Silent prayer.

Leader: Lord, forgive us our lack of courage in witnessing for you.

All: Lord, hear our prayers as we offer them through Jesus Christ our Lord and Saviour. Amen.

BIBLE READING
Matthew 15:21–28

PRAYERS OF INTERCESSION

Leader: Father, we pray for the islands of Samoa and their people. We think of the islands that are easily accessible, which are inhabited and where the government and commercial life is centred. We pray too for those islands that are more remote, with their own natural beauty and simple lifestyle. We thank you, Father, because we realize that the needs of the Samoan people, found in our prayers of intercession, are so often a reflection of our needs too.

Voice 3: O God our Father, may the power of your Holy Spirit rekindle our hope and enable us to become messengers of the gospel in our own communities.

Silent prayer.

Voice 4: Prince of Peace, we pray for peace among nations so that all may live in unity and harmony. Teach us to uphold justice and be fair in our decision-making. We pray for all those whose lives are affected by violence and war crimes.

Silent prayer.

Voice 3: Loving God, help us to reach out to those who suffer hunger and poverty. We pray for those whose lives are affected by deadly diseases that are still without cure.

Silent prayer.

Voice 4: We call upon you, O God, as climatic changes increasingly affect all our lives, to make us aware of the causes and help us to find ways to preserve our precious environment.

Silent prayer.

Voice 3: We pray for your blessing on government leaders in their decisions and policy-making for the common good of your people. We pray for church leaders worldwide, that they may work in co-operation for the growth of your kingdom.

Silent prayer.

BLESSING

Leader: As we go from here, may our informed prayer lead us to prayerful action.

The amazing grace of the Master, Jesus Christ, the extravagant love of God, the intimate friendship of the Holy Spirit, be with all of you. Amen. (*2 Corinthians 13:14, THE MESSAGE*)

NOTE: THE KAVA CEREMONY

Before the narrator speaks, islanders (suitably dressed) carry in straw mats and a small table (such as a wicker or garden table) to hold the kava. Some fruits and/or a Samoan flag are put on the table. Quiet music could be played as this is happening.

As the narrator begins to read paragraph 3, the Chief (a village leader, who can be either a man or a woman) enters, carrying a kava cup (a coconut shell can be used) and sits behind the table. The Host Orator enters, carrying some roots (such as ginger) and stands to one side of the Chief. Villagers carrying flower garlands follow the Host Orator. The villagers stand or sit on mats near the Orator.

The visitors from Britain enter from the other side with suitcases or backpacks (and perhaps a small Union Jack).

The ceremony begins and appropriate miming actions are made as the speakers continue.

During the narrator's concluding speech, the villagers and visitors move towards one another. The flower garlands are presented and the luggage is carried by the Samoans as they all move off in a friendly manner.

9

HOLY SPIRIT, FILL US

Lebanon

BACKGROUND

Lebanon is one of the smallest countries in the Middle East, less than half the size of Wales; it is bordered by Syria, Israel and the Mediterranean Sea. Behind the narrow coastal plain are two high mountain ranges, and in spring it is possible to swim and ski on the same day.

Lebanon grows a great variety of fruit and vegetables and is famous for olive oil and wines. Natural resources include limestone, iron ore and water. There are a number of environmental concerns, including deforestation, erosion, quarrying and pollution. Agricultural products, light industries, tourism and other service industries are the mainstay of the economy. The capital, Beirut, is a centre for education in the Middle East and has a number of good universities and other educational facilities. It is an important medical, banking, trade, services and communications centre.

Lebanon is a democratic parliamentary republic that became independent in 1943. The President is a Maronite Christian, who appoints a Sunni Muslin Prime Minister, and the Speaker of the Legislature is a Shi'a Muslim. Lebanon was a founding member of the United Nations. Freedom of religion is enshrined within the constitution and Lebanon is the only Arab state that is not officially Muslim. Christians and Muslims participate equally in government and administration. Arabic is the official language but English and French are also used. The Lebanese flag comprises two horizontal red stripes bordering a white one with a green cedar tree in the centre.

Lebanon is an ancient Bible land; its name appears 75 times in the Bible. It is a land where the first Christians walked, and the people are proud of its long Christian tradition. The position of Lebanon on the eastern shores of the Mediterranean has drawn in a variety of groups who, over the last 3000 years, have left many sites of historic interest. The long civil war (1975–92), precipitated by the large influx of Palestinian refugees into the country and later the Israeli occupation of the lands of south Lebanon, has created many problems. To rebuild the country, the government has had to borrow large amounts of capital. The spending power of most people has become very limited. There are two groups—the very rich and the poor majority. Many young people have moved to the cities in search of better job opportunities.

WELCOME

Leader: Blessed be God, Father, Son and Holy Spirit, and blessed be God's kingdom now and for ever.

Voice 1: Come with me from Lebanon, my bride, come with me from Lebanon... The scent of your garments is like the scent of Lebanon. *(Song of Solomon 4:8, 11b, NRSV)*

Voice 2: The appearance of my beloved is like Lebanon, choice as the cedars. *(Song of Solomon 5:15b, NRSV)*

Voice 3: From Lebanon, land of the cedars, land of beauty and fragrance, as described in the Song of Solomon, we greet you, our sisters and brothers around the world. We welcome you with the traditional Lebanese words,

'Ahlan wa sahlan' [the 'h' is pronounced as in 'hello'].
These words are the abbreviation of a longer phrase,
which implies that when you visit me in my home or
country, you will find yourself among family and will
settle in a fertile land with no rough places. God has
blessed Lebanon with natural beauty and a temperate
climate. Its diverse inhabitants thus became generous
and hospitable people, equally welcoming to friend and
stranger.

CALL TO WORSHIP

Leader: We come together on this blessed day, thankfully
worshipping and praising the Lord. May we be filled
with the Spirit and rejoice. For the Lord is a great God
and a great King above all gods. Today, when you hear
God's voice, harden not your hearts.

Spirit of truth, source of all righteousness, giver of life
and present in all places, come dwell in us and cleanse
us of all our iniquities.

All: Lord, have mercy.

Leader: Sisters and brothers, come and rejoice with the women
of Lebanon who experience the joy of faith in Jesus
Christ and his Spirit of comfort in the midst of difficulties and tribulations.

All: Come, ever-present Spirit of truth, fill us and work
through us.

Leader: Come with the women of Lebanon who lost their
children in the defence of their land.

All: Come, ever-present Spirit of truth, fill us and work through us.

Leader: Come with the women of Lebanon who have experienced the bitter taste of alienation in their own land; who courageously and patiently suffered displacement till they returned home.

All: Come, ever-present Spirit of truth, fill us and work through us.

Leader: Come with the women of Lebanon who, during 17 years of ugly war, have suffered the most difficult circumstances and economic hardships.

All: Come, ever-present Spirit of truth, fill us and work through us.

Leader: Come with the women of Lebanon who repudiate all forms of oppression, violence and injustice, and who hold on dearly to the love, compassion and mercy of God.

All: Come, ever-present Spirit of truth, fill us and work through us.

Leader: Come, sisters and brothers, let us praise our heavenly Father in whom we live and move and have our being.
Led by the pioneer and perfecter of our faith, our Lord and Saviour Jesus Christ, filled with the Holy Spirit, the Lord the giver of life, the Comforter, let us sing unto his holy name, hallelujah!

All: Hallelujah!

PRAYERS OF THANKSGIVING

Voice 1: From the depth of my heart, O Lord, with the women of Lebanon, I give you thanks and kneel at your feet.

You have ordered the universe, you are the author of life, the source of goodness, the well of mercy, the giver of peace and healer of wounds. Thanks be to you.

Voice 2: From the depth of my heart, O Lord, with the women of Lebanon, I give you thanks and kneel at your feet.

When troubles overtook me and I thought my country would not see an end to the long war, you appeared from on high and wiped sadness and sorrow from my heart. You gave me a taste from heavenly joy. Thanks be to you.

Voice 3: From the depth of my heart, O Lord, with the women of Lebanon, I give you thanks and kneel at your feet.

When I lost a loved one or a home or earthly possessions, you taught me that life is only meaningful with you and in you. In you, my loss is gain. Thanks be to you.

Voice 4: From the depth of my heart, O Lord, with the women of Lebanon, I give you thanks and kneel at your feet.

When my children emigrated in search of education and employment, I felt lonely and forsaken. The world darkened before my eyes. But your Word accompanied and comforted me. I received hope when I heard your voice saying to me: 'Lo, I am with you always, to the end of the age.' Thanks be to you.

All: Thanks be to you, O Lord, because you have sent the Holy Spirit to comfort us and to intercede on our behalf. Amen.

PRAYERS OF CONFESSION

Leader: Our Lord God, Jesus Christ, we confess before you all our sins and wrongdoings that we have committed, knowingly or unknowingly. We have hurt you and added to your wounds.

We therefore ask for your mercy and earnestly beseech you to wash away our sins by your precious blood and restore to us your grace.

All: Have mercy upon us, Lord, when we confess our faults, and restore to us the joy of your salvation.

Leader: Hear a voice of Lebanon.

Voice of Lebanon: Lord God, we deeply regret the injuries and shameful acts committed in your sight by some of our people during the long and terrible years of war. Many were uprooted from their homes; others were kidnapped or killed because of their religious affiliation. Children were mutilated, women were raped, the elderly were insulted and property confiscated.

Lord, on behalf of your people, we plead for your forgiveness from the depths of our hearts. Your long patience and endless love for us are not overwhelmed by our sins and iniquities.

All: Have mercy upon us, Lord, when we confess our faults, and restore to us the joy of your salvation.

Leader: O God, we stand before you today, just as we are, asking your pardon. We have failed to seek righteousness and reconciliation. We have forsaken the sick and the suffering. We have ignored the refugees and the poor. We have not defended the oppressed. We have not preserved our environment. Accept our prayers as we repent of our sins against you and against each other. Help us to serve our neighbours as we seek to serve you. May the power of your Holy Spirit purify, sanctify and keep us.

All: Have mercy upon us, Lord, when we confess our faults, and restore to us the joy of your salvation.

PRAYERS OF INTERCESSION

Voice 1: We pray for Yasmina, a nine-year-old girl whose legs were amputated after she stepped on a landmine while playing with her friends in the fields. Experts say it will take more than 30 years to clear the legacy of 139,000 mines left behind in the lands of south Lebanon after 22 years of occupation. Yasmina wants to play outdoors with her friends now that they are free, but neither she nor her friends are allowed to do so.

Silent prayer.

Voice 1: Lord God, help them and fill them with your Holy Spirit and enable them to enjoy their childhood.

All: O Holy Spirit, renew us that we may ever more persevere in your love, faithfulness, justice and patience, and please you all the days of our lives.

Voice 2: We pray for Hilaneh and others like her all over the world, whose sons have been kidnapped and never seen again. These families do not know if their loved ones are dead or alive. We pray that, even after so many years, they will be restored to their families.

Silent prayer.

Voice 2: O Lord, fill us with your Holy Spirit, and help us to face the difficult realities of this cruel life and accept them in your name and for your glory.

All: O Holy Spirit, renew us that we may ever more persevere in your love, faithfulness, justice and patience, and please you all the days of our lives.

Voice 3: We pray for Leila, a young woman studying environmental science at university. Like many other countries, her country, Lebanon, the beautiful biblical land of the cedars, has been disfigured. The trees have been cut down, the mountains quarried, the sea and air polluted and rare animals hunted. The prophet Isaiah gave hope for the future: 'Shall Lebanon in a very little while become a fruitful field, and the fruitful field be regarded as a forest?' *(Isaiah 29:17, NRSV)*

Silent prayer.

Voice 3: O Lord, fill us with your Holy Spirit; give us wisdom to restore your world and bring balance back to Lebanon.

All: O Holy Spirit, renew us that we may ever more persevere in your love, faithfulness, justice and patience, and please you all the days of our lives.

Voice 4: We pray for Nakba, a young Palestinian girl born and still living in one of the many refugee camps of Lebanon. Her parents, who sought shelter in this warm-hearted country, are thankful to the Lebanese people for accepting them and many other generations of refugees, for more than half a century. Surely it is time for them to return to their rightful homes. This is their great longing. They, and countless refugees in other countries, have waited too long and the world seems to have forgotten them.

Silent prayer.

Voice 4: O Lord, fill the decision-makers of the world with your Holy Spirit. Give them your wisdom and insight to see the truth, work for peace and establish justice.

All: O Holy Spirit, renew us that we may ever more persevere in your love, faithfulness, justice and patience, and please you all the days of our lives.

Voice 5: So many educated young people of the Lebanon are leaving and emigrating to greener pastures because of the economic and political instability in the region. Will they not hear the words of Jeremiah: 'Will a man leave the snow of Lebanon which cometh from the rock of the field? Or shall the cold flowing waters that come from another place be forsaken?' *(Jeremiah 18:14, AV)*

Silent prayer.

Voice 5: O Lord, may your Holy Spirit so fill the Christians of the Middle East, from whence came the first disciples of Jesus, that they remain as custodians and witnesses of your teachings in these lands.

All: O Holy Spirit, renew us that we may ever more persevere in your love, faithfulness, justice and patience, and please you all the days of our lives. Amen.

Silent prayer.

Leader: Lord, hear our prayers.

BIBLE READING
Acts 2:1–4

PRAYER

Leader: O Holy Spirit, the Comforter, who is one with the Father and the Son, you spoke through the prophets of old, and descended upon the apostles in tongues of fire; you filled the saints with holiness and granted them wonderful gifts. We beseech you to fill us with grace, enlighten us with divine light and empower us with the fire of your love. Renew in us the spirit of good works and grant that we may have everlasting life in you.

All: Amen.

BIBLE READING
Luke 1:26–38

PRAYER

Leader: Hear this prayer from Lebanon.

Voice of Lebanon: Lord Jesus, you have walked our land with your disciples. You have been to Tyre and Sidon and accompanied your mother, Mary, to Cana. She, the greatest among women, observed and obeyed. She whom all generations shall call blessed did not abandon the disciples, and was with them when they received the news of your resurrection and the power of the Holy Spirit in the upper room. Grant that we, the women of Lebanon, may overcome all life's difficulties. Help us to remain faithful mothers and guardians of the faith, seeking to preserve the wholeness and sanctity of our families.

All: Amen.

BIBLE READING
Galatians 5:22–23

The Leader and nine other readers group themselves around a large potted cedar, olive branch or other evergreen. Each in turn proclaims her fruit as she hangs an appropriate symbol on a branch, then all slowly and quietly return to their seats. Alternatively, candles or tea lights could be lit.

Leader: The fruit of the Spirit is…

Readers 1–9:   Love
Joy
Peace
Patience
Kindness
Goodness
Faithfulness
Gentleness
Self-control

Leader: Against such things there is no law.

PRAYERS OF DEDICATION

Voice 1: Lord God, lover of humankind, you sent the Holy Spirit to the apostles. We beseech you to fill us with the Holy Spirit so that our hearts and minds shall be enlightened and we may understand your will for our lives.

Voice 2: Holy Spirit, fill us with your wisdom and light so that we may discern the way of truth, oppose darkness and conquer hopelessness. Enable us to be loving and kind to others.

Voice 3: Holy Spirit, touch the young people of our lands. Direct their lives in ways of peace and tolerance, to enable them to control aggression and anger, yet achieve their dreams and ambitions. Enable them to discern the real spirit behind all the temptations they encounter— especially through the media, which infringe upon their lives and culture. Help them not to falter and fall, but to remain faithful, generous and gentle.

Voice 4: Holy Spirit, surround the elderly of our land with a halo of kindness and joy, so that their children and grandchildren will be drawn to them and learn from them to rely upon your living word now and for coming generations.

Voice 5: Holy Spirit, inspire the hearts and minds of those in government. Fill them with mercy, kindness, generosity and wisdom. Guide them to act justly and preserve human rights, especially for children who are in need of shelter, protection and access to proper education.

Leader: Together let us commit ourselves to walk according to God's guidance.

All: Create in me a clean heart, O God,
and put a new and right spirit within me.
Do not cast me away from your presence.
And do not take your holy spirit from me.
Restore to me the joy of your salvation,
and sustain in me a willing spirit.
(Psalm 51:10–12, NRSV)

BLESSING

All: Holy art thou, O God.
Holy is the Most High.
Holy is the Everlasting.
Have mercy upon us.
Have mercy upon us.
Have mercy upon us. Amen.

Leader: The creative power of God go with us.
The compassionate love of Jesus go with us.
The driving force of the Spirit go with us,
as we follow our calling to link God to his people.

© MARJORIE DOBSON

10

WOMEN SHAPE THE FUTURE

Panama

BACKGROUND

Everyone has heard of Panama hats and, more importantly, the Panama Canal—the marvellous piece of engineering, completed in 1914, that links the Atlantic and Pacific Oceans. Few of us know much about the country. Panama, almost the size of Scotland, forms a narrow bridge that joins North and South America, where the wildlife of the two continents meet and intermingle.

Panama is a beautiful land with dense tropical rainforests, deep rivers, cool mountains and an extinct volcano. The lovely coastal areas and the many small islands are a paradise for the tourist and far removed from the busy commercial life of the capital, Panama City, and the Canal Zone.

From the 16th century, Panama was exploited by Spain; much of the ancient culture was destroyed and many of the indigenous people died. Pirates also raided towns and cities. The country was often ravaged by storms. Through all this the Panamanians managed to preserve many art treasures and memorials, and rebuilt their lives and homes again and again.

In 1821 Panama became a province of Columbia but finally attained complete independence in 1903. This independent republic is a nation of contrasts. There is a woman President and, in law, women are regarded as equal with men—but in day-to-day life, old attitudes and values prevail. Many women are inhibited by the traditions and taboos of culture and religion. Improved education, more contact with the USA and the emergence of women's groups are helping to establish women as full citizens in home, workplace, church and community.

Panama is a mainly Christian country—85 per cent Roman Catholic, 15 per cent Protestant.

As we recognize that women have shaped the past, let us pray that, with our sisters, God will help us to shape the future—the future when God's justice and truth will fill the world.

WELCOME

Leader: Greetings! Welcome to the Republic of Panama, centre of the world, heart of the universe, in the name of Jesus, our Saviour and King! We invite you to join us in worship.

Now let us greet each other as they do in Panama: 'Buenas' [pronounced Bway-nas].

All: 'Buenas.'

Leader: Hear the voice of Panama.

Voice of Panama: The Republic of Panama is an isthmus between the Pacific and Atlantic Oceans. It is a land of opportunities with its privileged geographical location, different eco-systems and various ethnic groups. The word Panama suggests 'an abundance of butterflies and fish'.

Panama City is the capital of both the Province and the Republic of Panama. The Panamanian landscape is attractive with its forests, beaches, mountains, rivers and many species of flora and fauna. Museums and parks, and buildings of colonial and modern architecture can be found in its towns and cities. The most famous landmark of all is the Panama Canal. All of this is evidence of the country's great diversity.

Panama is a cosmopolitan country of different races, religions, cultures and languages. Spanish is the official language and English is widely spoken, along with other ethnic languages. The Caribbean influence is very noticeable because people from the islands laboured in the construction of the Panama Canal.

CALL TO WORSHIP

Leader: Almighty and loving God, we bless and glorify your holy name. You are the Alpha and the Omega, the beginning and the end. We draw near, asking for your blessing and giving thanks for your love, grace and mercy.

O God, unite our hearts as we meditate upon your love. Give us a deep desire to serve you with true reverence and devotion. Help us to acknowledge your presence at all times and in all circumstances.

Loving God, you have made yourself known to many women and have answered their prayers. We come in faith, as they did, confident of your help. Shape our lives according to your will.

PRAYERS OF THANKSGIVING

Leader: O God, we thank you for your glory in the morning and your abiding Spirit in the quiet darkness of the night. Grant us your peace and protection as we offer our thanks through Jesus Christ our Lord and Saviour.

All: Hear us, O Lord.

Voice 1: We thank you for the freedom to worship you. We are grateful for those who inspire and encourage us. We thank you for the gifts and talents of our children and for the opportunities to nurture and encourage them.

All: Hear us, O Lord.

Voice 2: We ask women throughout the world to join with us, the women of Panama, as we rejoice and give thanks for the beauty of our country. We thank you, divine Creator, for the diversity of our people and culture.

All: Hear us, O Lord.

Voice 3: We thank you for the vital commercial and international links that the Panama Canal provides. We remember with gratitude the thousands who laboured to construct this marvel of engineering.

All: Hear us, O Lord.

Voice 4: We thank you for women who are willing to unite to press for necessary changes in their communities, churches and schools. We thank you for women in leadership among the rulers of the nations.

All: Hear us, O Lord.

PRAYERS OF CONFESSION

Leader: Loving God, have mercy on us as we bring our failures, faults and selfishness to you. Forgive us for trying to solve our problems on our own. Help us to lay aside all evil desire.

All: Father, forgive us and grant us your peace.

Leader: Forgive us, divine Creator, that we have taken your creation and your kingdom for granted. You have given us a beautiful land and plentiful harvest but we are aware of having squandered these resources.

All: Father, forgive us and grant us your peace.

Leader: Compassionate God, forgive our foolish ways. Forgive us that we have not played our part in society. Forgive us that we have not been good stewards of all that you have given us.

All: Father, forgive us and grant us your peace.

Leader: Women have played a progressive role in shaping their countries over the centuries. The 20th century was punctuated by unprecedented changes, revolutions and innovations. Despite disturbing setbacks, perhaps the most persuasive lasting transformation in many parts of the world has been the emergence of women as a major presence and force in public life.

Today, we reflect upon the richness and diversity of women's experiences, past, present and future. We learn about their struggles and accomplishments in their daily lives. Knowledge of the past reinforces the promise of advancement for women and their societies in this new millennium. Our perspectives, which are constantly renewed through faith and prayer, open our eyes and extend our horizons. They shed light into the darkness of our fears and sorrows, our shame and pride, and fill us with joy and hope. Despite the immensity of the challenges, the faith of women is helping to shape the future of the world.

BIBLE READING
Numbers 27:1–11

Leader: The daughters of Zelophehad spoke out about the inheritance of lands, and a legal dispute was later solved. This encourages us to turn to God in all circumstances. The world needs to recognize God's moral law and to seek his guidance. Let us pray.

All: O God, give us unity, determination, faith and hope to bring our problems to you, so that we may receive help and courage to make the necessary changes in all aspects of our lives—economic, social, moral and spiritual. Let us strive in all our relationships to work with God for change. Amen.

BIBLE READING
John 20:1–18

PRAYERS OF INTERCESSION

Voice 1: All-powerful God, who equips us for ministry, we pray that you will continue to guide all women of faith. May we, by our teaching and example, help to shape the future. Lord, in your mercy...

All: Hear our prayer.

Voice 2: Risen Christ, in the same way that Mary Magdalene took the good news to the disciples, we pray that we too will be faithful witnesses to your living presence. Give us courage to accept the challenge of discipleship, and shape us in your service as you did the women of Galilee. Lord, in your mercy…

All: Hear our prayer.

Voice 3: Living God, in our daily walk we pray that the Holy Spirit will be our guide. Help us to yield to his leading, knowing that, as our friend, he will provide all that is necessary for us. May our love grow and may we be equipped to encourage and nurture others—our family, neighbours and friends. Lord, in your mercy…

All: Hear our prayer.

Voice 1: We pray for women leaders in Panama, especially those within the government, and for all women in leadership throughout the world. May they exercise justice and equality at all times. Lord, in your mercy…

All: Hear our prayer.

Voice 2: O God, we ask that strength and spiritual knowledge be given to all parents to bring up children in the faith and as responsible citizens. Lord, in your mercy…

All: Hear our prayer.

Voice 3: We pray for those who are suffering from hunger, poor housing, unemployment, loneliness and sickness, and for those in prison. We ask you to strengthen and guide all who minister to them. Lord, in your mercy…

All: Hear our prayer.

Voice 1: We pray for teenagers, that they will find employment. Grant them grace to resist all the temptations of youth. Lord, in your mercy…

All: Hear our prayer.

Voice 2: We pray for all married couples. May they be faithful to each other in every circumstance. Lord, in your mercy…

All: Hear our prayer.

Voice 3: We pray for women and children. May their lives be free from domestic and sexual violence. We pray too for those who are elderly. May we value their experience and wisdom, and endeavour to meet their needs. Lord, in your mercy…

All: Hear our prayer.

Voice 1: We pray for an end to discrimination in education, jobs and leadership. Lord, in your mercy…

All: Hear our prayer.

Voice 2: We pray for prayer groups in Panama and in other parts of the world, who intercede for the needs of others. Strengthen our faith, O God, that we might be messengers of your peace, love and justice. Lord, in your mercy…

All: Hear our prayer.

Silent prayer.

Leader: Lord, in your mercy…

All: Hear our prayer.

SHAPING THE FUTURE

Voice 3:   Pottery, one of the oldest crafts in the world, is made in Panama. It is shaped by hand or on a potter's wheel, using clay or other materials. Although the various items differ in style, colour and size, all are useful and valued. In the same way as the potter moulds the clay, the Holy Spirit moulds us for service, and we become 'special' in God's hands.

Leader: In scripture we read, 'But we have this treasure in clay jars, so that it may be made clear that this extraordinary power belongs to God and does not come from us.' (*2 Corinthians 4:7, NRSV*) Let us say together…

All: But we have this treasure in clay jars, so that it may be made clear that this extraordinary power belongs to God and does not come from us.

Leader: Let us pass a piece of pottery around to remind us that useful containers are made from ordinary materials.

Small earthenware plates or pots are passed around the congregation, while quiet music is played.

Leader: Women mould the future daily. When we awake in the morning, we are engaged, whether voluntarily or involuntarily, in shaping the future with the people who cross our paths. Beginning in their homes, moving out to their communities, workplaces and churches, women participate in educating by guiding, informing and instructing with actions, words and unconditional love. These are all part of our daily mission. Let us pray…

All: Dear Father, we thank you for the example left to us by women like the daughters of Zelophehad. We seek to be like Mary Magdalene and the other women who followed Jesus closely as his disciples. We recognize that we are as earthen jars, holding a treasure that is meant to be shared with all whom we meet. Use us, as you will, to extend your kingdom here on earth. Amen.

BLESSING

Leader: Now to him who, by the power at work within us, is able to accomplish abundantly far more than all we can ask or imagine, to him be glory in the Church and in Jesus Christ to all generations, for ever and ever.

All: Amen.

★ ★ Also from BRF ★ ★

QUIET SPACES

Prayer interludes for busy women

PATRICIA WILSON

The intimate relationship with God you've yearned for is well within your grasp, despite the chaos of juggling multiple roles, deadlines and commitments. This book can help you to use even a few stray minutes as an opportunity for a 'prayer interlude', calming the mind and listening for God's still, small voice in the midst of the tumult around you.

Each 'prayer interlude', which can be completed in as little as five minutes, offers a calming passage from the Psalms, a prayer meditation, a thought from the words of Jesus, and an exercise to help readers as they go back into the busyness of the day.

ISBN 1 84101 339 0   £5.99

Available from your local Christian bookshop or direct from BRF using the order form opposite.

ORDER FORM

REF	TITLE	PRICE	QTY	TOTAL
339 0	*Quiet Spaces*	£5.99		

POSTAGE AND PACKING CHARGES					
order value	UK	Europe	Surface	Air Mail	Postage and packing:
£7.00 & under	£1.25	£3.00	£3.50	£5.50	Donation:
£7.01–£30.00	£2.25	£5.50	£6.50	£10.00	**Total enclosed:**
Over £30.00	free	prices on request			

Name _____ Account Number _____

Address _____

_____ Postcode _____

Telephone Number _____ Email _____

Payment by: Cheque ❑   Mastercard ❑   Visa ❑   Postal Order ❑   Switch ❑

Credit card no. ❑❑❑❑ ❑❑❑❑ ❑❑❑❑ ❑❑❑❑   Expires ❑❑ ❑❑

Switch card no. ❑❑❑❑❑❑❑❑❑❑❑❑❑❑❑❑❑❑

Issue no. of Switch card ❑❑❑❑   Expires ❑❑ ❑❑

Signature _____ Date _____

All orders must be accompanied by the appropriate payment.

Please send your completed order form to:
BRF, First Floor, Elsfield Hall, 15–17 Elsfield Way, Oxford OX2 8FG
Tel. 01865 319700 / Fax. 01865 319701 Email: enquiries@brf.org.uk

❑   Please send me further information about BRF publications.

Available from your local Christian bookshop.   BRF is a Registered Charity

brf

Resourcing your spiritual journey

through...

- Bible reading notes
- Books for Advent & Lent
- Books for Bible study and prayer
- Books to resource those working with
  under 11s in school, church and at home

- Quiet days and retreats
- Training for primary teachers
  and children's leaders
- Godly Play
- Barnabas Live

For more information, visit the **brf** website at **www.brf.org.uk**